Praise for *Jesus in the Power of Poetry*

"In the power of poetry we encounter another Jesus: the storyteller, the cultural catalyst, the prophetic empowerer, the mystical liberator. Hopefully this endeavor will help to redeem Jesus from the cultural conditioning of Greek metaphysics and king-like imperialism. Hopefully it will also provide glimpses on how the original followers experienced the living Jesus, thus challenging and inspiring us today how to follow Jesus more authentically."

> —**Walter Wink,** Professor Emeritus of Biblical Interpretation,
> Auburn Theological Seminary, New York, and author of
> *The Human Being: Jesus and the Enigma of the Son Man*

"This creative book represents a bold and imaginative unpacking of the core theme of Jesus' preaching: the inbreaking (or revealing) of the Kingdom of God. Blessed with the gift of Diarmuid's poetic insights the reader sees beyond many of the culturally encrusted gospel stories. The result is an understanding of the subversive power of Jesus' message as relevant today as it was then. As a preacher, I found this book very helpful for homilists seeking new insights to help them communicate God's cosmic purpose regarding a new kind of 'companionship of empowerment.'"

> —**Michael H. Crosby, O.F.M.Cap.,** author of *Paradox of Power,*
> *Can Religious Life Be Prophetic?* and *Solanus Casey*

"Diarmuid O'Murchu introduces us to Jesus the storyteller, the one who through everyday experience places before us the opportunity for embodied revolution. O'Murchu himself is one of the great storytellers, and this book takes us on a journey fueled by theological creativity and expressed in engaging and challenging language. By being drawn into the language we are exposed to new possibilities and expanding visions."

> —**Lisa Isherwood,** Programme Director of Theology and
> Religious Studies at Winchester University, U.K., and
> author of *Liberating Christ* (1999) and *The Fat Jesus* (2008)

"This is a real gem! For too long we have thought that prose and theology could get us there, but O'Murchu has discovered what ancient religion knew to be true: the great mysteries must be left evocative, infilling, and endlessly mysterious — and poetry alone is fit for that task. You will ⸺ n sure!"

> —Richard Rohr, O.F⸺ plation

D1159012

"The metaphysical language of the Greeks, the dualism of body and soul, the imperial Roman law, a prescientific cosmology, and so many other impositions of our church's tradition have almost totally erased the dangerous memory of our master, the man of Nazareth. Jesus has been sent back to the heavens, and we lost the one we can follow, a radically human being. Diarmuid O'Murchu, in the companionship of the best of Christian scholars, invites the reader to *Catching Up with Jesus*. I joined him in his first study in which he searched to restore 'the radiant humanity of Jesus as the human face of God.' On the road to this rediscovery, Diarmuid felt that language, even in a storytelling form, falls short for imagining the subversiveness of Jesus. In *Jesus in the Power of Poetry*, we meet the rebellious Jesus, the mystic at heart, a poet who breaks open a congealed political-religious system to reveal a radical new way of being human by entering into God's birthing of a new kingdom, a kingdom not of power but of empowerment. The author takes the reader along on a discovery of this 'companionship of empowerment,' guided by the rebel of Nazareth. His poetry, like Jesus' parables, is 'unashamedly human, earthly and secular,' challenging the reader to sit at the table of radical inclusiveness. The well-documented introductions of the chapters, evoking different aspects of Jesus' life and ministry, help the reader to overcome what seems at times to be shocking affirmations about Jesus and his discipleship of equals. The remedy of such a shock treatment is to let Jesus and his companionship be fully human, and hence divine, something that a poet can allow to happen. 'The poetic character lives in gusto; poetry should surprise by a fine excess and not by singularity' (John Keats)."

— **Lode Wostyn C.I.C.M.**, Manila, Christologist and author of
Doing Christology: The Re-appropriation of a Tradition (1990)

"What an exciting exploration! O'Murchu reaches into meaningful territory: where poetry touches the dangerous subversiveness of Jesus and helps us appreciate the radiant humanity of Christ. While rational, linear approaches to spirituality have their place, they fail to resolve the mysteries of suffering and death. With buoyant creativity, the author takes us beyond institutional, patriarchal systems and into the poetic realm that delights, illuminates, and offers shining new possibilities."

— **Kathy Coffey**, author of *Hidden Women of the Gospels*,
Women of Mercy, and *The Art of Faith*.

JESUS IN THE POWER OF POETRY

JESUS IN THE POWER OF POETRY

A New Voice for Gospel Truth

DIARMUID O'MURCHU, M.S.C.

A Crossroad Book
The Crossroad Publishing Company
New York

The Crossroad Publishing Company
www.cpcbooks.com
www.crossroadpublishing.com

© 2009 by Diarmuid O'Murchu, M.S.C.

All rights reserved. No part of this book may be reproduced, stored in a retrieval system, or transmitted, in any form or by any means, electronic, mechanical, photocopying, recording, or otherwise, without the written permission of The Crossroad Publishing Company.

In continuation of our 200-year tradition of independent publishing, The Crossroad Publishing Company proudly offers a variety of books with strong, original voices and diverse perspectives. The viewpoints expressed in our books are not necessarily those of The Crossroad Publishing Company, any of its imprints or of its employees. No claims are made or responsibility assumed for any health or other benefit.

Printed in the United States of America.

The text of this book is set in 10.5/14 Adobe Garamond. The display face is Futura.

Library of Congress Cataloging-in-Publication Data

Ó Murchú, Diarmuid.
    Jesus in the power of poetry : a new voice for Gospel truth / Diarmuid
O'Murchu.
        p.   cm.
    Includes bibliographical references.
    ISBN-13: 978-0-8245-2521-7 (alk. paper)
    ISBN-10: 0-8245-2521-3 (alk. paper)
    1. Bible. N.T. Gospels – Criticism, interpretation, etc. 2. Bible N.T.
Gospels – Poetry. I. Title.
BS2555.52.O48 2009
226′.06 – dc22

                                                2008043635

1   2   3   4   5   6   7   8   9   10   15   14   13   12   11   10   09

Contents

Acknowledgments

It feels as if this book has been fermenting for almost half a lifetime. Although I have long outgrown the literalist interpretation of Christian faith, inherited from home and early education, I still cherish the "solid" grounding that has sustained me and pushed me to explore anew the poetic horizons of the present work.

I want to thank in a special way, my seminary professors in Milltown Park in Dublin, Ireland, who both inspired and baffled me and above all else awoke in me a curiosity and hunger to probe the deeper recesses of my Christian faith.

That ongoing exploration has been enriched far beyond my expectations by kindred spirits from the United States to Asia, from Europe to Africa. Facilitating international workshops and conferences for the past twenty years has evoked feedback, affirmation, and critique, the richness of which I cherish with immense gratitude.

I am deeply indebted to my Filipino confrere and scripture scholar, Fr. Ben Alforque, M.S.C., whose meticulous reading of the manuscript not only helped me to honor truth in the Scriptures but also opened up other original insights to whet my poetic appetite. My thanks, too, to Fr. Pat Courtney, provincial of the Missionaries of the Sacred Heart in Ireland, for his ongoing support and encouragement.

Finally, my editor at Crossroad, John Jones, has been gracious in encouragement and support, both in this and previous books. And I never cease to marvel at the thoroughness and meticulous care that John Eagleson brings to his work as manuscript editor — what a gift to a publishing house, and to me as an author as well!

JESUS IN THE POWER OF POETRY

Introduction

For over forty thousand years the Australian aborigines have crossed a desert larger than the continent of the United States, rarely getting lost and surviving some quite harsh conditions. There are few visual clues they can rely on. They opt for something much more imaginative, a creative wisdom that has sustained them for thousands of years.

When they reach a water hole, they tell a story or sing a song. The song holds the clue that will guide them in the next stage of their journey. The song triggers a muscle memory, a kinesthetic wisdom that indicates what to do next. They get places by riding the song-lines (also known as dreaming tracks).

This navigational skill is stored not just in their collective psyche, but in their physical experience, an advanced form of instinctual knowledge. Each totemic ancestor is thought to have scattered a trail of words along the line of his footprints; virtually every rock, creek, and distinguished landmark in the country has been sung. Through the song (or the story), one can reconnect with the embedded, embodied wisdom. The song-lines are a lifeline with an enduring sense of wisdom and hope.[1]

Accessing the Gospels through poetry feels like a biblical version of the aborigine song-lines. Poetry makes accessible scriptural insights not immediately obvious to the prose medium. Poetry connects us more readily to the psychic dimensions of an oral tradition where stories (and songs) are the primary media that carry empowering meaning. The sense of awe and wonder, the evocative sense of challenge and shock, the emotional release of affirmation and empowerment — these are some of the dynamics of an oral culture that are often subverted in the prose rendering.

In the power of poetry, Gospel characters come alive in a whole new way. We begin to reclaim the subversive Jesus, prophetically empowering and mystically liberating. Hopefully we also understand anew how the original followers experienced the living Jesus, and this empowers us as disciples of the twenty-first century to embrace our faith afresh, with vigor, vitality, and a renewed sense of commitment and fresh hope.

Chapter One

It Happened Like This

The sources of poetry are in the spirit seeking completeness.
— MURIEL RUKEYSER

I began writing poetry many years ago. Many of the poems I have written over the years I keep in a private journal. They often describe times of struggle and difficulty, internal searching and seeking, deeply intimate material that I have shared mainly with my therapist and spiritual director.

I don't recall making a conscious decision to write poetry in order to resolve internal conflict. Intuitively rather than consciously I began to realize that I could articulate through the medium of poetry those struggles that were not easily translated into rational discourse. The poems did not necessarily resolve my difficulties. Rather they enabled me to embrace and hold my personal dilemmas in a more gentle and insightful way, in a way that made it easier for me to live with some of life's great challenges.

Nor did it ever dawn on me that I should analyze in greater depth what was going on in those times in which I committed my internal process to poetic expression. It felt like the right thing to do, and I did it. Writing poetry brought a sense of relief, an inner calm. But of course, it was much more than that: poetry became the medium through which grace touched and healed my inner hurts and pains. It served as a kind of thread in the weaving on a loom that, time and again, gave fresh context, hope, and meaning to my life.

Gospel-Based Poetry

For several years colleagues and friends had been encouraging me to write a book exploring the meaning of Christian faith in the context of the new cosmology. Particularly in the United States many Christians struggled to harmonize their traditional faith in Jesus with the emerging insights and challenges of the new cosmology. Not being a theologian or scripture scholar, I did not want to take on a task that was outside the realm of my expertise, one that spiritually and intellectually I felt was best left to others.

But others were not forthcoming, and it became all too obvious that such a book was needed. Eventually, I assumed the challenge, and the final outcome was published in 2005 under the title *Catching Up with Jesus*.[1] It is probably the most adventurous and creative piece of writing I ever attempted.

Almost by accident, with little forethought or consideration, I one day decided to write a poem on the incident of the Pharisee and the tax collector in the temple. It was truly a "eureka" moment. The story came alive as never before. The characters became radiant and more transparent than I had previously realized. Most important of all I felt intense feelings around their respective realities. And spiritually I felt I was entering the mind of Jesus with a perceptiveness and sense of call that felt quite new.

During the following week I wrote ten poems related to different Gospel scenes. In every case new insights erupted; I was uncovering meanings and understandings I had never gleaned before. The Gospels were coming alive in a whole new way. In several cases, it felt as if I was really coming to know Jesus for the first time.

One aspect in particular was engaging my creative imagination: the subversiveness of Jesus. Poetry could honor the stretching of boundaries and the breaking open of congealed systems in a way that prose had not done for me. My excitement about the Kingdom of God and the call to follow Jesus with greater integrity and commitment gave my Christian faith a fresh and somewhat daunting impetus. Poetry was leading me on a spiritual pathway that was new and exciting, but also challenging and quite frightening at times. I guess I was undergoing a kind of transformation aptly described by Roger Housden:

> When the poet is reaching into territory that lies just beyond our conscious experience, we may shiver and not know why. We may not understand the sense at first, or even a second or third time; yet some tidal pull returns us to it again, and maybe again, till finally, perhaps, some magic slips open the knot, and we and the poem stand revealed. In this way, too, poetry is an agent of transformation.[2]

In my revamped story of Jesus, as narrated in part 3 of *Catching Up with Jesus,* I conclude each episode with a poem. I wanted to add more poems but on reflection decided to contain my enthusiasm. I now found myself resorting to poetry every time I was trying to discern the deeper meaning of a particular text or anecdote in the Gospels. I was convinced, and still am, that poetry can break open the power of God's word in a way that far exceeds what we access through the medium of prose.

Subliminal Meanings

I don't wish to excessively analyze what is going on for me. Rather I want to relish, in joy and gratitude, what I have discovered through the medium of poetry. Undoubtedly, I am touching into, and helping to unravel, subliminal undercurrents, and I guess these will become more transparent as time unfolds. I am happy to wait and see what will happen.

It feels relevant (and probably important), however, to share with the reader two insights, two connecting links, that seem to illuminate the deeper meaning of what I have been discovering. One is psychological in nature, and the other has to do with scriptural foundations. Many scholars alert us to the power of sacred texts to awaken and uncover meanings that transcend what the literal text describes. Our rational world tends to prioritize that which we can check and verify objectively, yet our experience consistently reminds us that the rich texture of life often embraces a great deal more than our rational logic can accommodate.

First, there is the psychological dimension. As a psychologist, I have long been attracted to the Jungian notion of the *collective unconscious* and its illumination through major *archetypes*. (I describe what this word means in chapter 2.) I have come to realize that objective rational knowledge always falls short in terms of true meaning, and correspondingly the archetypal is what provides (for me at least) a far deeper and more satisfying explanation.

Commentators on John's Gospel have long encouraged believers to honor first the symbolic meaning of the text, and only then adopt the literal interpretation. From a poetic perspective it seems to me that the symbolic meaning is the primary one throughout the four Gospels. Symbols point us to the deeper mystical layer that I call the archetypal, and numerous poems in this collection touch into that depth of reflection and discernment.

Our rational culture tends to dismiss the symbolic and archetypal as vague and fuzzy, too esoteric and fanciful to be taken seriously. When applied to Jesus in the Gospels — for me at least — it is the archetypal that illuminates the radiant humanity of Jesus as the human face of God. One begins to see why the more rational search for the historical Jesus has never really satisfied either the scholar or the spiritual seeker, precisely because it has underestimated, and often ignored, the archetypal context.

Second comes the challenge of interpreting scripture. A few years ago, I attended a workshop by Neil Douglas Klotz, one of a number of contemporary scholars striving to uncover the Aramaic Jesus.[3] Although the Gospels are written in Greek, Jesus, at least in the rural settings of first-century Palestine, would have spoken in Aramaic. It is probably impossible in our time to decipher which passages in the Gospels were initially spoken in Aramaic and which were uttered in Greek.

Douglas-Klotz claims that Greek and Aramaic are very different languages in their ability to express and communicate messages. Greek is a very precise, brief, a cryptic kind of language. Aramaic is much more ornate, elaborate, and polysemous. Where Greek can convey a message in a few words, Aramaic is likely to use many. More significantly, the worldview of classical Greek times is quite anthropocentric in focus: humans are what matter primarily. In the Aramaic worldview, reality is seen primarily as cosmic and planetary.

Obviously, these are generalizations that need to be further nuanced. However, we are encountering a hermeneutical question with implications for Gospel study and the discernment of scriptural meaning. And it seems to be a relatively new field of study requiring a great deal more research. If Douglas-Klotz is broadly correct in his claims, then we are encountering further evidence for what may be coming to light when we access the Gospels through poetry rather than prose. We may be uncovering a deeper layer of cultural insight more likely to reflect the archetypal flavor of the Aramaic rather than the linear and more rational tenor of the Greek.

The Poet in Each of Us

There may or may not be a scholarly rationale for accessing the Gospels through poetry. That will become only clear as others explore this medium to uncover the truth of our sacred texts. I offer my initial attempt in the hope that it will inspire and encourage others to make their contributions. I suspect all of us will be the richer — humanly, spiritually, and scripturally — for embracing this endeavor.

I am not offering this collection of Gospel poems simply for prospective poets. It is for all readers — Christian or otherwise — who are inspired and challenged by the Jesus story. For me, poetry has brought alive that seminal story in a radically new way. My hope and prayer is that it will be the same for each reader of this book.

Chapter Two

Poetry Unlocks Deeper Meaning

There are many pressures to quiet the text, to silence the deposit of dangerous speech, to halt this outrageous practice of speaking alternative possibility. The poems, however, refuse such silence. — SARAH CLASSEN

Prose serves the primary purpose of the rational in the desire to keep our analysis and explanation objective, verifiable, precise, and quantifiable. In the realm of prose it is much easier for the human to have a sense of being in control of the data. Poetry invites a more expansive, nondiscursive embrace of reality. In a word, poetry guarantees a more direct access to the realm of mystery.

These are some of the added dimensions the poetic mode is likely to illuminate:

+ Poetry is porous, incorporating a range of possible meanings, whereas prose favors more monolithic interpretations.

+ Poetry is more likely to unveil a multifaceted understanding of life and reality. In poetry the interpretative lens is wider. The poet can embrace larger horizons of perception while also plumbing greater depths of meaning.

+ When we engage the poetic process, the symbolic is likely to outwit the rational.

+ Poetry also helps to transform the rational in the direction of the archetypal and the mystical. The poet engages life on a multidimensional level.

+ Poetry is an art form with particular affinity to the use of imagination and the wisdom of intuition.

+ Poetry can entertain and honor ambiguity and paradox, which, in many cases, prose tries to resolve through logic and rational analysis.

+ Poetry has more unfiltered access to the experiential domain of emotion and feeling, and this is often reflected in the resonances and rhythms of the poetic structure.

+ Poetic license offers a freedom to speak the unspeakable, uncover what has been subverted, illuminate the invisible, and give voice to dimensions of life that tend to be subjected to invisibility and inaudibility.

Poetry Illuminates Archetypal Truth

The triumph of the rational is deemed to be a central and essential feature of our developed Western culture. The more we can verify scientifically and quantify for practical use the more we feel secure and sure about the ground upon which we stand. The success of our technology, on the one hand, and the intellectual superiority of rational discourse, on the other, assure us that this is the way to deal with reality. Not everybody agrees, and the prevailing rational culture is quite adept at restricting the alternative voices to more confined spaces.

Those who seek more than the rational have the comfort and assurance of religion. It helps us to make sense of things when the rational fails to deliver on its promises for progress and fulfillment. And religion is particularly useful where rationality fails to resolve the irregularities of pain, suffering, and tragedy in the world. One day, the rationalists claim, we will conquer these bizarre forces, and then we can dispense with religion.

But religion itself is also becoming highly problematic for many people, as highlighted in two quite different but related contemporary analyses.[1] On closer examination, we see that the monotheistic religions particularly (Judaism, Christianity, and Islam) are solidly rooted in rational wisdom, drawing heavily on the metaphysics of classical Greece. Much more appealing to the religious imagination of our time is the revival of *spirituality*. Despite its rather amorphous and at times contradictory articulations, spirituality speaks to the contemporary soul more profoundly and authentically than a great deal of formal religion.

Even those who explore the emerging spirituality often overlook one of its more intriguing and complex ingredients, namely, the *archetypal realm*. Anthropologists have noted this undercurrent in numerous indigenous cultures, ancient and modern, as highlighted in the twentieth century by Jungian psychology. Academic scholarship is reluctant to engage with this wisdom and in some cases openly ridicules those who explore its significance. Rationalism will engage only with what is deemed acceptable by its own terms of reference; it can be quite brutal in seeking to undermine and overthrow alternative insights.

Archetypes are patterns of meaning, psychic blueprints embedded in the creative vacuum of the universe, informing field influence in the direction of growth and wholeness. Archetypes cannot be known in themselves, but they may be accessed in the imagination through myths, symbols, rituals, the arts, dreams, and poetry.

In this definition, archetypes belong first and foremost to the cosmic creation itself, as a set of energy patterns that are manifest in field influences; this is a relatively recent field of study, the interface of physics and psychology.[2] Energy is itself

infused with a capacity for meaning and a sense of direction toward greater co-
herence and complexity. Humans appropriate the archetypal wisdom, not merely
because of some dynamics at work in our brains, but because our entire psychic
selves are always intimately connected with the source of our becoming as cosmic,
planetary creatures.

All the great religions embody archetypal meaning and content, but it is often
subverted and even corrupted by religion's favored adoption of linear thought and
rational discourse. Archetypes, however, exhibit a strange and powerful sense of
resilience. As James Hillman and other scholars highlight, archetypes seem to have
a kind of life of their own. They are particularly resistant to the controlling desires
of major institutions, religions included.[3]

Archetypal Awakening

How archetypes infiltrate human culture is vividly illustrated in Dan Brown's con-
troversial book, *The Da Vinci Code,* a work of enormous archetypal import for our
time.[4] Torn to shreds by its critics, the plot of the book is full of historical inaccura-
cies, with various totally unsubstantiated claims made by the author. Dan Brown
has consistently retorted that for him the book is merely a *novel,* a literary genre
that justifies the kind of liberties he has taken.

For millions around the word, *The Da Vinci Code* has been a gripping and
intriguing read. Some attribute this to an ingenious plot, others to a witty and
lively style of writing, others to the aroused curiosity concerning who actually
committed the murder of the museum curator with which the story begins, while
for others it is the provocative suggestion that Jesus and Mary Magdalene were
a married couple. These are all conscious explanations and in no way illuminate
the subconscious allurement. Readers become gripped by the power of a literary
plot that actually transcends the plot itself. It is this psychic hook that explains the
popularity of *The Da Vinci Code,* but very few analysts have even suspected such
profundity. Strangest of all is the fact that Dan Brown, the author, was not even
aware of the archetypal depths he was plumbing.

The central character in *The Da Vinci Code* is the Great Earth Mother God-
dess. There are nineteen substantial allusions to the Goddess in the book, with
consequent insights related to the Holy Grail. This is not merely religious fanta-
sizing on the part of Dan Brown. What we are encountering is a powerful cultural
archetype, which is quite volatile in our time. At its core it not just a desire to re-
claim the long subverted wisdom of the feminine (in women and men alike), nor
to expose the undermining hostility of Christianity toward the feminine (a task

that Dan Brown carries out very effectively), but *to reclaim the nourishing womb of our fragmented, exploited earth body.*

As the earth body becomes more depleted and oppressed by the brutal com-mercialization of our time, in our collective subconscious we begin to feel the precariousness of our collective situation. From within this space of collective trauma, archetypal wisdom arises, an urgent call from the Great Mother to wake up to what is really happening. Paradoxically, we humans give more attention to archetypal meaning than we care to acknowledge. And the more rational we strive to be the less attention we are likely to give.

The dilemma I highlight is clearly illustrated in the case of the movie version of *The Da Vinci Code,* touted to be one of the big movie hits of 2006. While many people around the globe flocked to see it because of the book's record-breaking sales, many came away disappointed. The movie failed to capture the gripping attention of the book. Why? Because the central message of the book was diluted almost to the point of invisibility!

To deflect the objections of the religious world, which had made the book so controversial, the moviemakers, in dialogue with Brown, decided to delete as much as possible the material on the Great Goddess. Only a few references occur explicitly in the movie, and these are so subtle one could easily miss them. The movie is a disaster *because it failed to honor the archetypal message of the book.* Not for the first time rationalists failed to comprehend deeper meaning, in this case, an archetypal awakening carrying a distinctive urgency for our time.

Is There a Christian Archetype?

Ever since the launch of the search for the historical Jesus in the late nineteenth century, scholars have detected a strange ambivalence whereby the more we estab-lish historical facts the more we seem to lose something of the spiritual appeal that Jesus has exerted throughout the two thousand years of Christendom. The great Rudolf Bultmann tried to resolve the dilemma by prioritizing *the Christ of faith,* while the radical Canadian scholar Tom Harpur suggests that we declare the his-torical Jesus to be nonexistent and focus solely on *the archetype of the Christ* from which the story of Jesus is borrowed in the first place.[5]

Among contemporary scholars addressing this dilemma, I find the seminal work of Walter Wink, *The Human Being: Jesus and the Enigma of the Son of Man,* to be singularly superior.[6] Beyond the leading theories of our time that tend to iden-tify the ideal human in terms of biological determinism or sociologically in terms of robust rational individualism, Wink seeks to explore the exemplary human in a way that honors transcendent dimensions (which I name as the planetary and cosmic aspects), while in no way denying the vulnerabilities and limitations of our daily human struggles. How these radically differing characteristics can be integrated into a meaningful synthesis is exemplified uniquely in the earthly life of Jesus, and thus it becomes a model for all Christians to embrace and appropriate.

But the archetypal significance is not confined to the earthly life of the historical Jesus. It also embraces every historical epoch in which God was becoming incarnate in human life. Thus it did not begin with the historical moment of Jesus of Nazareth, but rather with the original emergence of the human species some seven million years ago.[7] If we embrace the theological conviction that God is in solidarity with creation throughout its entire emergence, then God was fully present to, and unambiguously involved in, our human becoming in its initial emergence. God has been incarnating in the human throughout all human history, and not just within the Christian time frame of the past two thousand years.

Moreover, the revelation of God in the face of the human has been unfolding throughout every significant breakthrough of our long evolutionary story: upright walking, tool making, language acquisition, ritual, art. In all these developments the grandeur and creativity of God become more transparent. And the entire evolutionary process comes to fulfillment in the incarnation of God in the person of Jesus (for Christians) and in other incarnational embodiments we encounter in the other great religions (the avatars of Hinduism, bodhisattvas of Buddhism, prophets of Islam, shamans of various indigenous religions, diviners in the African religions).

The Kingdom of God as an Archetypal Icon

For Christians, this long process of incarnational maturation reaches a climax in the life and ministry of Jesus. The outcome is encapsulated primarily in what the Gospels describe as "the Kingdom of God," renamed in the present work as "the companionship of empowerment" (see chapter 3). A great deal has already been written on this subject, and while many scholars acknowledge the complexity and depth of the concept, few have attended to its archetypal significance.

Jesus serves as the first disciple for a universal cosmic, planetary truth that is greater than the individual Jesus, embracing an enduring context out of which the historical Jesus developed and appropriated a particular historical identity. The companionship of empowerment is primarily about God's reign in creation (i.e., God's radical grace-filled presence in the whole universe). In the life and ministry of the historical Jesus it assumes a more definitive expression, which is itself an articulation of the divine incarnational radiance in each and every human who has ever lived on earth.

In the present work I use poetry to uncover the subverted tradition of the companionship of empowerment, and the radical new way of being human that constitutes our human flourishing in God's New Reign. The Jesus that comes to light and the discipleship envisaged in following Jesus begin to look very different from what is portrayed in popular Christianity, but also significantly different from the divine-human figurehead we encounter in the theories and findings of formal Christian scholarship.

The Christian archetype is not easily defined; we risk creating yet another dogma! It can be described, however, as a type of tapestry into which are woven all of the following features:

+ Jesus is an incarnational revelation of God embracing, celebrating, and affirming the incarnational flourishing of humanity throughout the seven-million-year span of our evolutionary existence on planet earth.

+ For Christians, Jesus is the human face of God, embracing and revealing the "fullness of life" (John 10:10) that all are called to emulate. Here I follow C. F. D. Moule, who distinguishes between the Greek *bios* (biological life) and *zoe* (the fullness of life).[8]

+ Jesus, in the power of unconditional love, is a primordial embodiment of relational humanity, forever calling us to come to fuller life through right relating.

+ Jesus is a subversive prophet who frequently turns conventional wisdom on its head (as in the parable stories). In the vivid words of Thomas Sheehan, "The kingdom was his madness."[9]

+ As a prophetic subversive storyteller, Jesus embraces an alternative wisdom to that of the rational, prosaic rhetoric of the dominant culture.

+ Jesus is a human-divine exemplar of empowerment, denouncing all expressions of imperial power and delivering a liberating praxis of "power-with" rather than "power-over."

+ Jesus is a missionary catalyst who prioritizes the disempowered and disenfranchised, human and earthly alike.

+ Jesus is an archetypal healer of persons and systems alike—a healer rather than a preacher or teacher.

- In fidelity to the enlarged horizons of archetypal breakthrough, Jesus espouses religion with a lightness of being and instead invests heavily in an empowering and liberating spirituality.

This is the Jesus who announces the revolutionary program of the companionship of empowerment with the clarion call: Set my people free. Hopefully, the poetic reflections that follow will contribute to the flow of that freedom, not just for God's people, but primarily for Jesus himself! After two thousand years of imperial Christendom, Jesus too deserves to be set free!

Chapter Three

Poetry and the Story of Jesus

We have only the word, but the word will do. It will do because it is true that the poem shakes the empire, that the poem heals and transforms and rescues, that the poem enters like a thief in the night and gives new life, fresh from the word and from nowhere else. —WALTER BRUEGGEMANN

The trouble with some of us is that we have been inoculated with small doses of Christianity which keep us from catching the real thing.
—LESLIE DIXON WEATHERHEAD

The Gospels are written in Greek, representing the ancient culture from which we have inherited the wisdom of the logical, the rational, and the tendency to juxtapose reality into binary pairs of opposites. Greek thought is analytical, cerebral, and quite compatible with the rigors of the scientific method.

Having translated early Christian experience into the Greek mind-set — which was very different from the Hebrew way of understanding — the nascent Christian faith was subjected to further institutionalization in its adoption of the imperialism of Roman culture. Early in the fourth century, Constantine declared Christianity to be the official religion of the Roman Empire. From then on the structural context of Christian history heavily reflected the modus operandi of imperial Rome.

Greek and Roman Conditioning

Those two influences, Greek and Roman enculturations of the message and vision of Jesus, rooted the Christian faith in the emerging culture of the time and certainly made it more widely accessible. In doing so, however, we paid a high price, a compromise too far, one that has been named by many scholars throughout the twentieth century. We heavily domesticated the prophetic message of Jesus, we tamed the dangerous memory, and we anesthetized the subversive wisdom that constitutes the heart of Gospel hope.

Consequently, we have robbed the parables of their subversive impact and camouflaged the empowering breakthrough of the miracles by turning them into magical acts justifying divine power. The radical new way of being human, revealed in and through Jesus, has been severely curtailed in order to prioritize divine kingly power. Not surprisingly, perhaps, for during much of Christendom, Jesus was depicted as a white European, respected and worshiped as a respectable middle-class citizen.

The greatest calamity, however, was the neglect of *the archetypal,* the Jesus who represents and reveals the divine-human emergence and its foundational rootedness in the cosmic-planetary web of belonging. All the messianic projections, infiltrated with the desire for patriarchal dominance, seriously undermined the archetypal significance. Only when that is duly acknowledged can we hope to reclaim an understanding of Jesus that will honor the deep integration of both the human and divine in Jesus—and in each one of us.

In a word, we have made the Gospels safe, well subjected to the rational mind of male clerics, who have molded the Gospel to bolster their own imperial view of reality. The outcome predictably is heavily anthropocentric (with the cosmos and planet earth receiving little or no attention), predominantly male-oriented (women are rarely named in the Gospels), strongly focused on a powerful king-like Jesus (the very thing Jesus consistently denounced), and overly preoccupied with the divinity of Jesus (a subconscious desire to validate male imperial power).

Poetry has no place in this dispensation. The poet is deemed subversive in patriarchal territory and is unlikely to survive there for long. Rational prose keeps the allegiance as close as possible to literal interpretation, unambiguous meanings, and a clear chain of command from the top down. Even Jesus is kept in his place, in accordance with the protocol of loyal and faithful obedience.

The Core Archetypal Truth

But there is another face to Jesus, and scholarship for well over the past hundred years has been resurfacing this alternative revelatory figure. This is the Jesus much more transparent to the liberating power of poetry. This is the Jesus rooted in the prophetic inheritance of the Jewish people but also saturated in the power of *Sophia Wisdom.* We encounter a dangerous Jesus who topples the mighty from their thrones and in the power of parabolic speech turns convention on its head, time and again. This is the Jesus of that empowering dispensation which the Gospels describe as the "Kingdom of God," probably one of the most subversive strategies ever recorded in human-divine history.

This is the core archetypal truth of the Gospels. Many, if not all, scripture scholars will agree with this statement, but go on to offer a vast range of explanations. Several years ago, Norman Perrin described the concept as a "tensive symbol" whose set of meanings can be neither exhausted nor adequately expressed by any one referent.[1] This is a complex, multifaceted phenomenon, what N. T. Wright calls "a grand narrative," although he confines the context to the biblical themes of the exile and restoration of Israel.[2] The tendency to short-circuit this foundational meaning — of broad scope and complex significance — has bedeviled scholarship for several centuries and is now evoking a greater thoroughness and transparency as we seek to discern the authentic truths of our Christian faith.

Both C. S. Song and Schubert Ogden challenge the scholarly tendency to overidentify the Kingdom with the life and ministry of the historical Jesus. It encapsulates a larger and more complex landscape. "Strictly speaking," argues Song, "Jesus did not bring God's Reign into the world, for it was already there. What he did was to engage people in the manifestation of it, to enable them to know it is there, and to open their mind's eye to see it."[3]

In more philosophical terms, Schubert Ogden also views the New Reign of God as extending beyond the boundaries favored by Christian scholars: "What Christian revelation reveals to us is nothing new, since such truths as it makes explicit must already be known to us implicitly in every moment of our existence. But that this revelation occurs does reveal something new to us in that it is the occurrence in our history of the transcendent event of God's love."[4]

The actual historical meaning is further jeopardized by the language we popularly use. In English the word "King-dom" reflects masculine values, while the Gospels, written in Greek, use the word *basileia,* which is feminine. Scholars assume that Jesus spoke Greek and would probably have used it in debate with the scribes and other intellectuals of the day. However, his home language was Aramaic, the language he would have used in his ministerial discourses especially among his followers. In Aramaic, the word for Kingdom is *Malkuta,* which is feminine, and in the corresponding written version (Hebrew) it is rendered as *Mamlaka,* which is also feminine.

The preponderance of feminine words suggests that Jesus used the word "Kingdom" with a very different meaning from our conventional Western understanding.[5] Even a translation like "New Reign of God" (used by several contemporary scholars) probably does not do justice to the original meaning. Whereas "Kingdom" denotes royal power and domination, privilege, exclusion, and hierarchical control, the feminine versions used by Jesus denote something much more egalitarian, liberating, and empowering, a quality of leadership that enables and empowers others to take the next steps.

An Empowering Horizon

One of the most daring and visionary retrievals of the foundational vision was published in 1986 by a little-known American scholar, Thomas Sheehan.[6] Sheehan claims that in adopting the rubric of the Kingdom, Jesus was seeking to transcend all religion and empower people toward life in abundance (John 10:10), to be realized in the context of their daily secular reality. For the greater part most other commentators have concentrated on highlighting the limitations of our conventional understandings and our failure to see the patriarchal, regal underpinnings then and now.[7]

Catholic scholars (such as Fuellenbach) often present what to me seems a compromised vision.[8] Seeking to honor the priority of the Kingdom and its extensiveness beyond the church, they still seek to defend the position that despite all its limitations, the church is, and must be seen as, the primary embodiment of the Kingdom on earth. The evidence of history does not sustain this conviction, and it carries little weight for more enlightened Christians in our time. That Jesus envisioned faith communities to subsequently embody his vision is beyond question, but something akin to basic Christian communities, rather than an institutional church, is probably what he had in mind.

Among scholars, the Kingdom of God continues to be a field of intense study and research. Paradoxically, it does not feature strongly in the formation programs offered either in theology schools or in seminaries. The ambivalence of many centuries still seems to undermine our resolve to follow Jesus more fully. Or it might be natural human reluctance to take on a vision that could lead us to places we would rather not go!

The Language Itself

To resolve the dilemma of our ambivalence we may need to do something a good deal more drastic: change the terminology itself. As many philosophers indicated throughout the twentieth century, language dictates and limits consciousness. Language controls our lives to a far greater degree than most of us are aware. A new language is often necessary to move us in the direction of new possibilities.

For many years, I have encountered people, particularly women, who find the term "Kingdom of God" alien and oppressive. Many people have never had a direct experience of living under the governance of a king (or queen). And many educated people today readily see the archaic imperialism that inherently belongs to such language and the imagery it begets. Perhaps the time has come to get rid of the terminology itself.

And what would we replace it with? John Dominic Crossan offers a creative alternative: *the companionship of empowerment.*[9] Certainly this is what all the parables are pointing toward. And if we take the miracles as the first signs of the Kingdom happening, then the miracle stories also support this renaming. It also honors something of the original language used by Jesus, particularly the Aramaic *malkuta,* which literally translates as "the right to rule," but the underlying connotation (signaled by the feminine word) is that of the power of vision and leadership that empowers others toward a more empowering future.

The life and ministry of Jesus has as its primary focus, the disempowered of the day, the underclass, the oppressed, those marginalized and victimized by the dominant regimes, both political and religious. Contemptuously, they were called "the people of the land," later labeled by Rome as bandits, thieves, and brigands, those perceived as social or religious renegades because they did not follow the full rigor of social and religious custom. Six specific regulations applied to these people: entrust no testimony to them; take no testimony from them; trust them with no secret; do not appoint them guardians of an orphan; do not make them custodians of charitable funds; do not accompany them on a journey. It was regulations such as these that Jesus forthrightly condemned and subversively sought to reverse. Anything disempowering people had to be got rid of.

The companionship of empowerment also challenges and transcends the competitive individualism so endemic to our time and quite alien to the time and culture of Jesus. The empowerment envisaged in the life and ministry of Jesus is that of setting relationships right, co-creating communities and networks through which we incarnate transformative justice, healing and forgiveness, empowering love and enduring liberation. The countercultural call is not that we look to others to do it for us (the kingly, hierarchical model), but that we mutually empower each other to do it together — for each other and for the earth we inhabit. This is also the vision of the Beatitudes, the radical option for which Jesus lived and died.

Throughout the present work, I occasionally refer to the "Kingdom of God" but as far as possible I will adopt the newly suggested terminology of "the companionship of empowerment." In making that change, I don't believe I am in any way betraying tradition or tampering with sacred writ. Rather, I am striving to reclaim something closer to the originality and dynamism of what Jesus was on to in the first place, a vision that Christians of every age and culture are invited to embrace. With this new language and the vision it embodies, Christianity stands a much better chance of becoming once more the *dangerous memory* it was always meant to be:

> Not living in a spiritual world, whether "beyond time and space" or beyond the "world's" reach; but as living in a sacramental universe, where the signs of God's providential care are everywhere to be recognized, learned from, and received with thankfulness. Not as a closed society determined by rules and excluding boundaries, but as a community which seeks above all else God's priorities, in which forgiveness is experienced, which is often surprised by grace, and which knows well how to celebrate God's goodness in the openness of table-fellowship and love of neighbor.[10]

Chapter Four

Empowerment beyond the Lure of Kingship

The poet does not come to have a say until the human community has engaged in its best management. Then perchance comes the power of poetry — shattering, evocative speech that breaks fixed conclusions and presses us always toward new, dangerous, imaginative possibilities.   —WALTER BRUEGGEMANN

About seven thousand years ago, kings evolved for the first time. The major distinction between kings and other clan or tribal leaders is that kings were considered to be the primary embodiment of God on earth. Just as God ruled from the sky above, kings came to be regarded as the primary creatures through which the rulership of the divine would be known on earth. Divinity and kingship became virtually synonymous.

All the major religions embrace this notion of the king as the primary icon of the divine on earth. In all the great scriptures we find allusions to God's kingly rule, and even in our own time kings carry semidivine significance in a number of developed cultures, e.g., the United Kingdom, Thailand, Japan. All the great religions also embrace the notion of priesthood, but in nearly all cases, the priest is subject to the king, and while the priest is considered a mediator between humans and the gods, the king seems to be beyond the need for such mediating, being himself essentially divine.

Throughout all religious history, divine breakthrough or intervention is expected to happen through some new quality of kingly presence. Therefore, the awaited Messiah of the Jewish people would appear as a king. In anticipation of this we see the Gospel writers (Matthew and Luke) trace royal genealogies (Matt. 1:1–17; Luke 3:23–38), acknowledging, as many scholars highlight, that Luke seems more concerned about Jesus' human lineage than his royal pedigree. In an age of many claiming to be messianic figures from God, one of the surest ways to check their authenticity was to establish if they belonged to a royal line. If they did, then their authenticity stood a much better chance of being verified; if they did not, they could quickly be dismissed as forgeries.

The historical accuracy and veracity of such genealogies seems not to have been in question, either in early Christian times or since then. One gets the impression that this ethos of kingly might and dignity still influences our understanding of God and the divine; in our hymnology we still use songs acclaiming God and Jesus to be of kingly stature, power, and glory. This is a cultural assumption that seems to be in urgent need of fresh appraisal, requiring a much deeper sense of discernment.[1]

Allegedly, the Jewish people are still waiting for the Messiah to come in some kind of kingly glory. And Christians are waiting for a king-like judge to appear "at the end of time." Scripture scholars and theologians, especially priests, still try to decipher some level of meaning in these ideas, while growing numbers of lay people consider them to be ridiculous. For many Christian women, the notion of God as a ruling king is perceived as authoritarian and oppressive. Increasingly, the kingly icon and model is falling into disrepute, catching up eventually with the political demise of kingship in most contemporary cultures.

Most serious of all, from the Christian perspective, is the growing awareness that Jesus totally disassociated his life and ministry from the cult and culture of kingship. That understanding of God he turned totally on its head. Moreover, he seems to have done so in a very subversive and highly offensive manner, effectively dislodging all semblance of kingship and embracing unreservedly *the companionship of empowerment.*

◆ ◆ ◆

The poems of this section offer a broad overview of how the projection of royal power influenced the people of Israel in their expectation of a messianic, king-like figure.

Poem 1: Walter Wink helps us to captivate that sense of expectancy in the midst of great social and political turmoil:

The world that Jesus entered was seething with human longings that showed in messianic dreams, millennial fantasies, apocalyptic desperation, mystical revelations, suicidal nationalism, religious critique and reform, reactionary rigidity, and a sense that time was collapsing, that the future was foreshortened, that the mystery of reality was about to be revealed. In such a milieu, the authenticity of Jesus was like a beacon that drew all mythological motifs to itself. Incubating in the womb of that period was God's rash gamble that humanity might become more humane.[2]

Poem 2: Matthew 1:1–17 and Luke 3:23–38 provide lengthy genealogies as evidence that Jesus was indeed a messianic figure, descended from a royal line, and consequently endowed with the divine power to rescue and save the people in such turbulent times. Obviously, the genealogies are not meant to be taken literally. Objective historical evidence would not have had the weight then as now. In all probability the Gospel writers, in compiling the genealogies, had little or no interest in historical verification. Had the writers not included such lineages, nobody would have taken seriously what later came to be known as the infancy narratives.

Poem 3: It looks as if the Magi (Matt. 2:1–12) were also coming with royal expectations, and they too experienced quite a degree of cultural dislocation, poetically captured by T. S. Eliot's *Journey of the Magi.* The kings came to celebrate a special birth, but as they return to the old familiar world, it does not feel the same anymore. Are they dealing with birth or death? This is often the question posed by a paradigm shift.

Poem 4: Even if the genealogies were true, they would have had little or no significance for Jesus. If Jesus did belong to a royal lineage, he clearly renounced everything it stood for by opting for the companionship of empowerment. And perhaps the most persuasive evidence for that claim is Jesus' choice to ride on a donkey, not a horse, on the last journey into Jerusalem (Mark 11:1–10; Matt. 21:1–9; Luke 19:29–38). Of all the subversive deeds Jesus did, this is the most provocative. It is a supreme insult to, and a total ridicule of, the culture of kingship. Subliminally, it is also an unambiguous empowering endorsement of the common people for whom the donkey is a primary symbol of their daily life and toil.

Scripture scholar F. Scott Spencer summarizes the scene in these words: "Jesus does not enter the holy city with pomp and circumstance: he commands no gilded chariot, or noble steed, nor is he carried on a royal litter or servants' shoulders. Rather he rides a humble beast of burden, befitting his affinity with the weak and lowly."[3]

Poem 5: The powerful myth of the royal divine rescuer prevailed and colors the apocalyptic literature especially in the book of Revelation, Mark 13, Luke 21, and Matthew 24. This melodramatic literature may have been largely inspired by the war of 66–74 C.E., which left Israel devastated, Jerusalem destroyed, and the temple demolished. Thousands were massacred.[4]

At the heart of the apocalyptic literature is the phenomenon of kingly power, extensively destructive, on the one hand, and paradoxically liberating on the other. When faced by hardship or persecution people often adopt a coping mechanism of fantasizing an alternative future; this helps to explain the wild, even bizarre, imagery of apocalyptic literature. The hoped-for freedom will be procured by a new imperial ruler, and Jesus comes to be seen as that new kingly liberator.[5] This is quite a different understanding from the Gospel vision of the companionship of empowerment, and hence the confusion that has dogged Christian hope over the centuries.

Poem 6: Finally, as kingship became identified with the imperial power of white Westerners (i.e., Europeans) so Jesus, in Christian art, tends to be portrayed as a white man with a distinctive European facial structure. This is a cruel betrayal, first, of Jesus' historical Palestinian origins; second, of his archetypal identification with humans throughout our evolutionary story; and third, of his solidarity with humans today — especially the suffering and marginalized — across the globe.

1. An Expectant Age

Years of conflict, turmoil and oppression, my people their spirits subdued.
And they longed for the grace of new freedom, as the prophets had said would come
through.
Both the land and its produce so cherished, was robbed from within and without.
Such taxes and tolls were demanded, left people with little to tout.

They conjured up visions to hope in, and fantasized what it would be like
To cast off the yoke of oppression and bask in the freedom of light.
But in seeking this new liberation, they anthropocized in extreme.
Placing trust in imperial forces that further would deplete their dream.

The system they much took for granted was corrupt in the heart of its core.
A new dispensation was needed, with justice and love to the fore.
The old expectations were weary like the systems that kept them in place.
And the false pride of this chosen people would never deliver true grace.

Empowered for a grounded engagement, the God with whom they'd co-create
Would stir up the forces of justice and proclaim a New Reign at their gate.
Some saw in the wisdom I offered that this would not challenge in vain.
And the movement it gathered momentum to become the new dream of my reign.

2. The Child of a Projected King

My people were brainwashed in kingly allure,
The victims of inner oppression.
Forever they looked to the forces outside
To rid them of pain and depression.
And highest of all was the God in the sky
Depicted on earth as a king.
Which forced them to bow their heads even more
And aggravate oppression's sting.

The child that was thought to bring hope as Messiah
Was labeled with kingly imprint.
It bored me to tears all the energy spent
In tracing my regal descent.
Hysterical hopes were staked on my fame
As the people colluded so widely.
My disciples, alas, were addicted as well,
To the throne of a king so unsightly.

The kingship of God is a fantasy fierce,
Deluding the people to see
That we displace the power in creation's allure
Where we worship a God that is free.
We're people of service with love to empower
Through meaning that comes from within.
It can never be gained by projecting outside
In guru or redeeming king.

3. Kingship in Crisis

They came to worship dignified, as kingly people tend to do,
The old familiar role time had instilled.
And dignity they brought, in act and gift alike
With everything in place, their task fulfilled.
But Emmanuel the infant threw back a wrenching smile
Recoiling from the dignity imposed.

Another dispensation here to lure the searching heart,
More dislocating than they could have supposed.

While pleased with their accomplishment and honors all conferred,
They found themselves going home another route.
They knew that things were not the same as when they first engaged
And they knew it was not Herod's hot pursuit.
Perturbed and disillusioned, could they retrace the star
'long the footsteps they had followed like a guide?
But the star had changed direction, and the night sky sang with joy
Casting spells upon an Orient gone wild.

People still kneel down and worship before the icon's lore
Admiring mythic glory from of old.
While Emmanuel the Adult has broken all the rules
In discipleship for justice, true and bold.
This embryonic figure, depicted in a child
Unsettles all of logic's microscope
And beyond the co-dependency, oft sanctioned by the myth
Lies the aperture for liberty and hope.

That primal birthing energy we all have undermined
While neglecting pregnant meaning to embrace,
Empowering us for justice, transformation is at hand,
In the healing power of God's salvific grace.
And fresh hope springeth fiercely while we forge the way ahead
As the Spirit of new life reclaims desire.
For the infant in the mythic cave can change the course of time
Through the adults who'll consume baptismal fire.

4. What's a King Doing on a Donkey?

The Passover feast was a crunch time; Messiahs pretending were rife.
And credentials for kingship were checking to ensure the divine would survive.
I felt I should do something drastic, this cult so perverse interrupt.
So I opted to ride on a donkey, declaring royal kingship corrupt.

Our kings always rode on their horses, the stallion a symbol of power!
But the beast of my people for riding was the donkey they used every hour.

For threshing, for ploughing, and for journeying, and chores by the dozen as well.
The donkey empowered their existence, a symbol one could not excel.

The regime of power is redundant, demolished as circles entwine.
The center empowers a new freedom with the donkey as icon sublime.
And the people cast garlands rejoicing, acclaiming that the God who sets free
From the power of the horsemen so brutal, it's the dawn of a new liberty.

They accused me of rousing the people. They said they were shouting too loud.
When the people befriend new empowerment, even stones hard as rock will cry out.
I headed straight up for the temple, the old dispensation locate.
And broke through their gross desecration, declaring new ways to relate.

The Gospels distorted the story, the task of empowerment subdued.
Unique among parable breakthrough, they cut out the poetry of truth.
Watch out for that king on the donkey, a symbol prophetic if rare.
Declaring that hope still has meaning for those with the courage to dare.

5. An Apocalyptic Ruler: You Must Be Joking! (Based Largely on Rev. 19:11–16, 21)

A nightmarish spot, that island of Patmos, as John fantasizes traumatic.
Mid feverish panic and violence so fierce, in battle with raging demonic.
And that heavenly horse alleging I rode, enveloped in heavenly glory.
I hope 'twas a stallion with plenty of guts, engaging in warfare so gory.

John says that my eyes were flaming with fire, overladen with crowns to adorn.
And he claims I was eager for full-bloodied war with dragons and beasts full of scorn.
The horses were white and the linen cloths, too, but dripping in blood ever crimson.
And out of my mouth a fine-sharpened sword, to complete so much trivial nonsense.

A tattoo on my thigh—whoe'er put it there—declaring my lordship so mighty.
And rule with a rod—pure iron at that—'gainst the whores and the beasts so
    unsightly.
I know persecution evokes in the poet the need to subversively vision,
But John's ruminations disastrously show the madness of violent confusion.

The horse of apocalypse in royal accolade has nothing to do with my vision.
And the lamb who was slaughtered I happily pass to the violence of patriarch's mission.

I rode on a donkey, my first beast of choice, my option for total nonviolence.
To carry the burden to make justice real and the echoes of warfare to silence.

Two thousand years later confusion prevails, mid violence with many addicted.
You oft compromise the nonviolent way, the collusion which power has inflicted.
The New Reign of justice I clearly proclaimed, a radical new dispensation,
Beyond the divisions of nation and race, lies the hope of a new liberation.

6. I Was Never White

I was never white to start with, endarkened by the sun,
My ancient roots from Africa I know them well!
And so do you! All of us were black to start with.
And, today, our ethnic origins are brutally suppressed
Mid tribalistic conflict and corruption running rife,
Zimbabwe's starving people; the Congo's bitter strife.
Despairing west to Darfur where oil might cost your life,
Infecting AIDS pandemic and some can't even drink
The streams of mass starvation leave little hope for strength.
This land of INCARNATION, it breaks my heart to see
That humans could have sunk so low in sheer depravity.
Let's stop the brutal savagery
And all the childish rivalry.
Together let's come home again
To the truth that sets us free.

I was never white to start with, and dearly loved the East
Adorned in multiplicity of faith and vision great.
The Hindus and the Buddhists, the Muslims and Bahai
The Chinese and the Indians, their lure we can't deny.
But the suffering of Burma, and the Tamil conflict torn
The peace they seek in Pakistan and hope for Vietnam lorn
I still hear cries of Khmer Rouge and Chinese brutal power
While Indonesia trembles, Tibet awaits its hour!
This land of INCANTATION, it breaks my heart to see
A culture rich in Spirit, yet much barbarity.

Let's stop the brutal savagery
And all the childish rivalry.
Together let's come home again
To the truth that sets us free.

I was never white to start with and always longed to visit
The lands not yet discovered in the West.
The forest of the Amazon, the mighty Inca tribe
And the early tribal settlers who loved their land with pride.
I want to seek forgiveness for those who used my name
To proselytize so brutally, to butcher and to maim.
And stand beside the rising poor who seek to liberate
Romero and the martyred ones upholding living faith.
This land of LIBERATION, it breaks my heart to see
How long it takes the rising poor to obtain true liberty.
Let's stop the brutal savagery
And all the childish rivalry.
Together let's come home again
To the truth that sets us free.

I was never white to start with and must ask the Europeans
To withdraw the white projections I've endured.
They Romanized my vision and imperialized my reign
And they colonized my glory to exert their power and gain.
But now it's time for reckoning with Europe in decline,
A church disintegrating, and Christendom is dying.
A time to grieve and mourn, a time to shed the leaves
Till Winter yields a future, what the Spirit yet perceives.
This land of much STAGNATION, it breaks my heart to see
So much resistance and denial, the old they can't let go.
Let's stop the morbid apathy
And all the childish rivalry
Together let's come home again
To the truth that sets us free.

Chapter Five

How God Gives Birth
to Empowerment

Poets speak porously. They use the kind of language that is not exhausted at first hearing. They leave many things open, ambiguous, still to be discerned after more reflection. They do not pretend to know the future, but offer the present as a shockingly open and ambiguous matter out of which various futures may yet emerge. —WALTER BRUEGGEMANN

The notion of God as ruler, as one who governs and controls like an earthly king, still dominates a great deal of popular religious belief and undoubtedly carries hope and promise especially for the poor, marginalized, and oppressed peoples of our world. To this extent, Karl Marx was spot on in describing religion as the opiate of the people.

It is also noteworthy that when people's material circumstances improve they often distance themselves from, and even abandon, the religion that sustained them, but with hindsight one can see that it also kept them co-dependent. As we adopt a greater sense of adult faith for adult people, we will need to outgrow, and eventually abandon, all the kingly imagery. It may have served the patriarchal culture of the recent past, but has little to offer for a more vibrant faith for the future.

As we let go the imagery of kingship, mediated through domination, control, power-over, co-dependency, we can adopt an alternative metaphor that is much more ancient in terms of spiritual belief and practice, and also much more empowering for the evolving spiritual consciousness of our time. I refer to the metaphor of *birthing,* initially born for me through an inspirational line from the writings of the thirteenth-century Dominican mystic Meister Eckhart: "What does God do all day long? God lies on a maternity bed, giving birth all day long."[1]

This is a metaphor we have known as a spiritual species for thousands of years, since long before formal religions ever came into being. As indicated in chapter 2 above, it carries substantial archetypal meaning for our time. The Great Goddess

45

of our Paleolithic ancestors was perceived as a woman of prodigious fecundity, birthing forth the stars and galaxies, the mountains and oceans, and every life form populating planet earth today. God, the great life-giver, in the pregnant power of creative Spirit, is probably the oldest and most enduring understanding of the Holy One known to our species. It carries deep archetypal meaning.

It strikes me that this is a far more dynamic and empowering metaphor for scriptural and theological discernment, one that honors wisdom of great age, speaks inclusively to men and women alike, and, for the purposes of the present work, illuminates the Jesus story in a far more liberating and empowering way than the wearied and oppressive metaphor of the ruling king.

This is the call of Grace Jantzen, and a number of other feminist scholars, to shift the emphasis from *mortality* to *natality*.[2] Salvation in the deeper archetypal sense does not come from the cult of sacrificial death, but primarily from the capacity for birthing forth new life. The infancy narratives, therefore, need to be approached afresh, not simply as a mythic tale about some kind of supernatural pregnancy, through a woman largely stripped of all her fertile female uniqueness, but as an archetypal statement of the God of prodigious birthing.

The Christian vocation begins to look very different. It is not primarily about repenting our failures as victims of a fundamental flaw that can only be rectified by an interventionist savior. Instead, we are called to become co-birthers with our birthing God for the ongoing evolutionary re-creation of God's world in justice, love, compassion, and liberation. Incarnation becomes an empowering and liberating dynamic, and Christians, instead of fleeing the world, are now challenged to embrace it in its full embodied existence.

◆ ◆ ◆

The poems of this section focus on the infancy narratives in the Gospels of Matthew and Luke.

Poem 1: We begin with Mary, the archetypal birthing mother, not the sanitized disembodied "virgin," robbed of her Palestinian historical grounding, where she would have had to be quite a robust, earthy person to survive the ordeals and hardships of the time.[3] This overspiritualized portrayal has also disconnected us from the earthy Jesus and a more grounded and contextualized base for God's immersion into our human reality. As the poet seeks to recover the true Mary, we obtain glimpses of Mary's own struggle, as a woman and mother, trying to make sense out of this strange child she birthed, nursed, and nurtured into adult life.

In adopting this approach, portraying Mary as a fully embodied human person, we begin to encounter the paradox that characterizes every expression of incarnation: the more radiant the humanity, the more transparent becomes the archetypal (divine) nature. In the case of Mary, this leads us first and foremost to seek connections with the ancient tradition of the Great Goddess,[4] rather than opting for the more esoteric, spiritualized dimensions of conventional devotion that in many cases undermine rather than enhance both the humanity and spiritual status of Mary.

Poem 2: Next we review the poignant story of two women — Mary and Elizabeth — living under the shadow of social and religious disgrace (Luke 1:39–56). For long, Elizabeth lived with the curse of being barren, making her not just an outsider in the community but one seen as somehow cursed by God with this terrible affliction of not being able to conceive. In the case of the young Mary, she is pregnant out of wedlock, a serious taboo in her day, one the Gospels rationalize at great length, providing instead a spiritual caricature that militates against the vibrancy and promise of incarnational breakthrough. Ironically, the incarnational import would be much more significant if we honored the possible illegitimacy of her pregnancy as authors like Jane Schaberg and Gerd Lüdemann invite us to do. Then, indeed, Jesus' solidarity with the sinner and outcast would be even more radiant.[5]

Poem 3: The actual birth of Jesus, apart from being a historical event (for which we have no specific material evidence), is also a call to each one of us to birth the inner child, that archetypal source that awakens wisdom and creativity for our life and mission as people invited and challenged to immerse ourselves in the companionship of empowerment.

Poem 4: And at every birth the archetypal "shepherds" are celebrating, being themselves disempowered (ritually impure) people in the time of Jesus: "Shepherds in the ancient world were typically associated with bandits, brigands, rebels and other troublemakers."[6] Women of poor means also worked as shepherds.[7] Their inclusion in the Christmas story is quite a subversive anecdote, but mild compared with the texts of John's Gospel, where Jesus is depicted as the Good Shepherd (John 10:1–18), a bold prophetic and subversive self-description rarely honored in the depictions of popular Christian devotion.

Poem 5: John's Gospel (2:1–11) opens with this amazing story of the wedding feast at Cana, loaded with subversive, symbolic intent. The six stone water containers were the kind the Jews used for ceremonial washing. For ceremonial cleansing, the Jews preferred water from stone containers rather than clay pots.

Imagine what would happen if guests wanted to wash their hands again: they would go to the water pots and find every one of them filled with wine! There would be no water for their ritual washing. In one unexpected moment, Jesus seems to be declaring all the former rituals and beliefs redundant and useless. The water is replaced with the new wine, for the new celebratory people of God! What a revolutionary moment!

Poem 6: Let's take the metaphor of birthing and new life into the depths of Mark's Gospel, embracing one of the most enigmatic parables in the New Testament: the cursing of the fig tree. Many scholars follow the line of William R. Telford, claiming that there is a strong significance in the fact that the account of Jesus' cleansing of the temple in Mark's Gospel (Mark 11:15–19) is sandwiched between the two sections of Scripture dealing with the fig tree (vv. 12–14 and 20–25).[8] Is this not a parable of Jesus declaring the temple itself to have outlived its usefulness and therefore no longer capable of bearing fruit for holiness and growth?

It has often been noted that the fig tree was a special sign of fruitfulness for Israel. Frequently, it was the tree from which the people brought the first-fruits to the temple. But now the vine and the wine flowing free are the fresh symbols for a newly empowering and liberating dispensation.

Poem 7: Wisdom is justified by her deeds! (see Matt. 11:16–19; Luke 7:31–35). Scholars such as Elizabeth Johnson, Elisabeth Schüssler Fiorenza, Denis Edwards, Ben Witherington, and many others suggest that the message of Jesus may be more deeply rooted in the Wisdom tradition of the Hebrew Scriptures than in the kingly or prophetic vein. By adopting the strategy of storytelling and apparently an extensive use of proverbs and pithy sayings, Jesus seems to be adopting both the strategy and outlook of the Wisdom literature.[9]

The people of his day, and especially the figures of authority, did not warm to this approach. They would have expected something more rational, formal, and authoritative from a messianic-kingly figurehead. The new wisdom, like the new wine, was turning their conventional world upside down!

1. *The Archetypal Mary*

CHORUS:
I am the Madonna who's black to the core.
And I birth forth a freedom that lasts evermore.

You have cast me in stone like a Queen of the Right,
A white European, so humble and trite.
From head to toe veiled, bizarre the décor,
You have robbed my uniqueness in Palestine's lore. CHORUS.

My birth was as simple and poor as the rest,
Begotten by God in the power of real sex.
No fancy angelic triumphalist hype
But tendering care amid my struggling tribe. CHORUS.

I grew up with stories of struggle and pain,
My people were waiting for God to regain
Our freedom from those who burdened our way.
So we eagerly waited for God's bright new day! CHORUS.

Messiahs by the dozen claimed they were the one.
Begotten they said by miraculous turn.
And my eldest darling decided he'd claim
To have been selected for messianic fame. CHORUS.

If only they knew what the background was like
Out of wedlock conceived — a merciless plight
And all that I suffered — so undignified
Suspecting all through a remarkable child. CHORUS.

He was restless and strange from a very young age
And questioned religion with the wit of a sage.
He traveled the world, to places on end
With a freedom in heart I could not comprehend. CHORUS.

He joined with a commune down near Jordan's shore
And a guy called the Baptist with prophetic lore
Marked him out for a mission I don't understand
My wild little lad and his apostolic band. CHORUS.

They say he worked marvels and preached like a lord,
And among the great leaders caused no little discord.
I never could answer when the neighbors did ask
The meaning and purpose of his missionary task. CHORUS.

It all turned sour after three years astream.
It seems he reaped havoc on the temple's regime.
By the time I was called, in a cruel twist of fame
He was dead on a cross; my God, what a shame! CHORUS.

For months, I kept out of the public domain,
But the women disciples kept calling my name.
And that woman from Magdala, she never gave up
Till the vision was grounded in a new Christian church. CHORUS.

I tried to support what the new group brought forth,
New freedom and peace, and some enduring hope.
We laughed and we suffered, yet knew it was right
While I never forgot my bright wayward child. CHORUS.

They say I was assumed to the heavens above
Once more robbing from me the earth that I love.
How I wish they would cherish my feminine truth
As a woman and mother to God's earthly rule.

    FINAL CHORUS:
    To the earth I belong like the Goddess of yore
    A radiant woman — but dark at my core!

2. Elizabeth and Mary: Pregnant in Strange Circumstances

Their stories intermingle and their shadows overcast;
Their memories are dangerous and must not be dismissed.
For one it is the barren curse
While the other's secret is much worse
Proscribed beyond all mention in the power of holy writ.

Elizabeth was barren, an affliction of the worst,
And would not reveal her pregnancy till she could disprove the curse.
But the dominating culture
Devouring women like a vulture,
Would be satisfied with nothing less than a male child of repute.

Rumor has it that young Mary out of wedlock did conceive,
A plight too grim to entertain with no hope of reprieve.
And a spiritual distortion
Blown well out of proportion
Subverted all her anguish and her brokenhearted truth.

But we glimpse the hidden story when the two meet face to face.
We will never know what they knew — a shared burden of disgrace.
But their stance is truly faithful,
And their gaze is ever grateful
To the one who lifts the lowly from the dungeons of despair.

They awaken for each other the liberating truth,
Holding healing and forgiveness in their pregnancies of hope.
Co-birthing with the Holy One,
Strangely sensing God's own will be done,
Embracing in each other's soul a world's waiting dream.

3. Birthing the Inner Child

Pregnant echoes rumble in a woman's fertile womb
As egg and seed ignite the Spirit's fire.
And nature weaves through slime and blood as God designed it so.
Arousing in the woman's womb new fruitfulness aglow
The home of God's own glory is erotic pure desire.

The mythic tale we sing about is archetypal lore,
With a virgin's awesome birthing in the middle of the night.
A womb-like cave the centerpiece with animals to greet,
While an archetypal Senex looks on but quite discreet.
And earth unites with heaven all adroit.

We love the childlike story of innocence and fun,
For children symbolize for us a promised future hope.
But an archetypal offspring carries paradox intact,
And to literalize the story distorts the holy tract
Of a mystery so luminous in scope.

In every sense, this is a child of human destiny,
Born forth in cosmic glory like us all.
He can challenge and inspire,
And can set our hearts on fire,
To embrace the inner child awakening every call.

The Bethlehem of folklore illuminates our way
In a cosmos so prodigious with new life.
And that's the invitation for every child to glow,
To engage God's full creation and release each pregnant flow,
So that peace and justice in our world thrive.

4. Could Shepherds Be Good?

Mid rocky cave and mountain trek, in season hot or cold,
In tranquil times, mid setting sun, or petrified when thieves would run.
I shepherded the little flock — to make a start in life.

I met my husband mid those rocks, attending sheep as well.
Despite the odds and ridicule, and little learning without school.
I shepherded the little flock — to keep the household going.

We both recall with quite delight that special scary starlit night
When a birthing mother refuge sought, in a rocky cave our hands had wrought,
Where I shepherded the little flock — in birthing young ones too.

She laid her baby in that trough; Dear God, it smelt and looked so rough.
Even shepherds rarely did resort, to desperate measures quick and curt,
Where I shepherded the little flock — and nurtured fragile life.

And years went by, my children grown. They don't shepherd as we did of old.
One now has joined a guru guide, from Galilee a shepherd's pride,
Where I shepherded the little flock — igniting hope aglow.

It pleased my heart to hear my son, tell tales of a "Good Shepherd" one.
A shepherd so described as GOOD; no one would use so nice a word,
When I shepherded the little flock — we were the underclass.

The Gospels often talk of sheep, those lost and found while vigil keep.
Don't glamorize our menial task. 'Twas rough, and tough, and full of risk,
When I shepherded the little flock — 'twas hard to hold our pride.

While now I savor better times, and seek the same for all.
Too many still are poor and stretched; with little hope, oppressed and wretched.
Let's shepherd them proactively, toward freedom and new life.

5. Water Jars Full of Wine

Plenty of water in plenty of jars,
Plenty to wash away the spiritual scars.
In the hope of obtaining a purified soul,
And placate the God who demands ever more.
And many just never achieved it!

They had water abundant for many a day
And washed themselves clean God's wrath to allay.
To be ritually pure was a major ordeal,
Affecting the body from head-top to heel.
Absorbed in a law of enslavement.

The stone-jars we'll put to alternative use
And forget about cleansing the holy refuse.
'Cause the prophets foretold the day of the vine
When the land would flow rich in the grace of new wine.
And the New Reign of God would receive it.

A new dispensation has now been declared
And the reckoning code is forever impaired.
Whether sinner or saint, whether washed or impure,
There's new wine for all, our hope to procure,
And the water jar now is a chalice!

Come drink from the feast of the fountain of life
For the banquet is open to all without strife.
There are no conditions, requirements of law;
We're God's blessed creation beyond basic flaw.
It's almost too much for our spirits.

Plenty of water in plenty of jars,
Plenty to wash away the spiritual scars.
But wine is for drinking to placate desire,
In the New Reign of God, we have hope to inspire,
The wine which we share in abundance.

6. The Cursing of the Fig Tree

There's fresh fruit to nourish those seeking true justice,
And it's not what the fig tree produces.
Instead it's the vine and what's crushed from the grape
And even the fig tree that grows in its nape,
Can't match the new wine flowing abundant.

The fig trees of Israel for long have sustained
Those charging their loot in the temple.
They rob from the poor, their God to placate,
For power and for profit they richly inflate,
While the fig tree has long ago withered.

The tree of the figs is the symbol of old,
Once helping to feed their starvation.
A new dispensation has now broken through,
A new way to worship — the temple adieu!
The death and rebirth of a people.

Before Nicodemus could answer the call
He sat 'neath the fig tree of legend.
He had to forgo what nourished his soul
And encompass the vine as the new way to grow.
Only then can he be a disciple.

It wasn't the fig tree I cursed on the way
But a parable story to waken;
Alerting those who resist how to change,
And embrace all outside who feel hungry and strange,
In the vineyard of fruitful abundance.

7. The Generation for Which Nothing Changes

The imagery is listless, a frozen frame in time.
For these people nothing changes,
Not even music rearranges.
They cannot wail to the grieving dirge,
They cannot dance to the music's surge.
In the comfort of complacency,
They must not be disturbed.
But the music ruffles constantly, inspired by Wisdom's urge.

While clinging to their comfort they cannot fail to note,
The Baptist eats so sparingly
While Jesus eats so daringly.
Their expectations all are shattered,
They thought they knew what really mattered.
In the comfort of complacency
New questions will disturb,
While the music plays another tune, inspired by Wisdom's urge.

Their world of convention is breaking at the seams.
Irrupting all around them,
An ageless reckless Wisdom.
A deeper truth invades their comfort zone
And another dispensation paves their way back home.
The comfort of complacency
Defies what they can fathom.
While the music that empowers anew evokes another rhythm.

They'll get there in the end of course,
But time is not to spare.
They need to start the grieving
And the dancing—if they dare!

Chapter Six

Hidden Years to Awaken Empowerment

The purpose of poetry is to explore rather than to explain, not so much to interpret as to intensify. A poet may not be able to save the world, but he can help to make it worth saving.
— LOUIS UNTERMEYER

The New Testament tells us little about the childhood, adolescence, and young adult years of Jesus. From a vast array of cultural studies on the living conditions of the times we can glean what it must have been like growing up in that environment. And we get sufficient hints from the Gospels to realize that the young Jesus was not a conformist, nor was he committed to local, national, or religious convention.

In all probability he was quite a rebel, at times causing his parents headaches, embarrassing his family, and perceived in the local community as someone quite odd.[1] The fact that he was not married marked him as a maverick, even in the eyes of some as a social traitor. He may also have traveled extensively, possibly as far as southern India, as suggested by the film *Aquarian Gospel*.[2]

His allegiance to the Jewish faith is particularly problematic. Indeed, it may well be accurate to depict Jesus, the teenage rebel, challenging, and even contradicting, the temple teachers. His disregard for laws of impurity and other aspects of his faith may have started quite early in life. Portraying Jesus as regularly attending the temple or synagogue probably says far more about the religious faith of scripture scholars than about Jesus himself.

Eventually, he got involved with millennial movements of his day. How many we don't know since the Gospels allude to only one, namely, the sect of John the Baptist. This might well have earned him the label of a New Age freak. And if the emphasis on the strict ascetic nature of John's group is correct, then there probably would have been major disagreements between Jesus and John's disciples. Finally, we need to include the possibility that Jesus was a mystic at heart,[3] and that it was this mystical depth that animated and sustained his bold, prophetic vision.

◆ ◆ ◆

In the poems of this section I want to give voice to those aspects in the life of the young, mystical, rebellious Jesus that the Gospel writers sanitized and made amenable for middle-class respectable hearers.

Poem 1: Those anticipatory years were probably quite turbulent, and already we sense the awakening power of the prophetic. The opening poem, therefore, presents Simeon and Anna (see Luke 2:25–38), two wise elders, inviting the reader/listener into an archetypal space, from which Jesus can be viewed in a more mystical and prophetic light.

The two central characters, Simeon and Anna, are classic examples of the archetypal Wise Old Man (Senex) and Wise Old Woman (Crone). Old age is a gathering-in time, holding the wisdom for the great transition from life to death. The archetype celebrates that which is new and fresh, epitomized particularly in the ability of the Senex to embrace fully (that is, integrate) the archetypal inner child.

The Crone is often described as the wisdom figure at the crossroads, so apt for Anna of the tribe of Asher, an excluded group in the political maneuvering of the time.[4] In fact, they each represent something of the crossroads, especially in their embrace of the messianic hope for a future more bright and promising than the oppressions experienced under imperial regimes.

Poem 2: Prophetic people rarely belong to conventional straight-laced families. The chances are that Jesus was quite a rebel from a very young age, openly disagreeing with, and radically questioning, many of the cultural conventions of his day, including his religion. The poet is not merely free to unmask this hidden, subverted portrayal, but also has a duty as a cultural catalyst to open up this alternative viewpoint. Only by embracing all such possibilities are we likely to honor the full incarnational significance of Jesus — then and now.

Poem 3: Like other teenagers of his day Jesus would have undergone the Bar Mitzvah rite of passage, which in all probability is the context for the events described in Luke 4:16–30. It is also quite likely that we are witnessing the rebellious young Jesus who uses the moment to disturb a few conventional truths. This might well have stirred up not merely the disapproval of the temple and synagogue authorities, but indeed their wrath as well.

Poem 4: From quite a young age, there is evidence to suggest that Jesus was uneasy about the temple and all it represented. His challenge to the temple teachers, recorded in Luke 2:41ff., might well have a historical foundation, a foretaste of what would happen frequently in Jesus' public life and ministry.

Poem 5: As Jesus moved into his twenties and showed no signs of marrying, he would have become the focus of much attention, and probably a great deal of gossip. As far as we can glean Jesus did not marry, not because of an ascetical dislike for sexuality or disregard for human intimacy, but rather as a protest against the prevailing culture of male domination.

If Jesus had chosen to marry, then he would automatically have been colluding with all the roles and values that upheld the dominant culture. In assuming the roles of husband and father he would have been endorsing the prevailing view, which regarded women as biological resources to fertilize the male seed and produce offspring for the man. Children he would have treated not as persons but as property. He would have seriously undermined his credibility relating to the companionship of empowerment by aligning himself with a system that considered *power over* the key value to be unrelentingly guarded, particularly through heterosexual marriage and the propagation of the family system.

Poem 6: Commentators tend to overspiritualize the story of the temptations of Jesus (Matt. 4:1–11; Luke 4:1–13). This cryptic narrative probably encapsulates many years of struggle and insight, an unfolding process of discernment in which Jesus is trying to figure out which options might best serve the companionship of empowerment, which was to become the core of the Gospel message.[5]

Poem 7: Popular Christian piety glorifies the holy family as a harmonious, God-fearing threesome, the perfect model for every earthly household. The historical reality seems to have been very different. The Gospels give a few, but significant, hints of the adult Jesus not at all at ease with his family (see Mark 3:31–35; Luke 11:27–28; 12:51–53). Even Mary, his mother, struggled to fathom the meaning of his life and mission; yet, it seems, she bravely stood by him till the end and supported the early disciples in the post-Resurrection period.

The critical issue here seems to be Jesus' unambiguous commitment to *the companionship of empowerment,* a new "family" dispensation characterized by radical equality and inclusiveness, unlike the patriarchal family system, which was the primary means for inculcating dominance, control, and exclusive male power. Jesus is not advocating that we hate our own kin — the Aramaic, *sena* (hate) has a root meaning denoting to strain, filter, clarify — but rather that we *love more* the newly enlarged family being invoked in his name.[6]

1. Blessed by the Wise Elders

Simeon and Anna advancing in their years
In the contours of the temple bide their time.
Imparting of their wisdom and blessing to support
What enables every child to reach its prime.

The Old Man of fulfillment, so mindful of his end,
Knows the inner child, of friend and foe alike.
With a heart so full of gratitude for life's abundant gift,
And a future in the promise of new life.

And the Crone, a rank outsider, of Asher's tribe up north
Transcending all the forces that divide.
This child, a one predestined, a force to reconcile,
And rid the world of all who like to fight.

Redemption of Jerusalem and Israel to console,
The elders guard our liminality.
The wisdom for the journey, from beginning to the end,
Is what elders have to bring abundantly.

2. Hidden Years to Mold a Maverick

The Gospels love to put things in gentle holy writ
Suggesting that I grew up aglow with saintly script.
They emphasize obedience, a loyal and faithful Jew,
Observing all the holy laws, religious through and through.
Suppressing that which truly made me real.

Our little home in Palestine, no different from the rest,
Amid the ups and downs of life we tried to do our best.
I did the things my siblings did and sometimes had to rue,
Being blamed the trouble-maker often had me in a stew.
And the Gospels have not much to say on that.

I was restless and contrary from a very early age,
So the legends on the family record.

And my parents did not like my desire to roam abroad,
To see the wider world, so elegantly charged.
And the Gospels have not much to say on that.

And they could not figure out my reluctance to engage,
Or get married as my peers were wont to do.
But that would curb my freedom and normalize my lot,
While the fire inside me burned to unfold another plot.
And the Gospels don't have much to say on that.

I baffled all around me when I joined the Baptist's group
Trying to live as an ascetic for the law.
And I also caused some panic amid the Baptist ranks,
Denying the holy value of these ascetic pranks.
And the Gospels have not much to say on that.

I fled into the desert to try to sort things out,
Get away from all the pressure in my home.
In the lonely inner struggle, I began to see the light,
Beyond human approval I had to do what's right.
Yes, the Gospels tell you something about that.

3. Bar Mitzvah Time:
My First Glimpse of Mission

Having thought long and hard, my vocation in life,
The call of the Spirit to listen.
I found myself opening the book of Isaiah
And was drawn to the place where 'tis written:

    CHORUS:
     You're called and anointed to bring to the poor
     The captive, the blind, and disheartened,
     A reign of empowerment, healing and hope,
     A new face of God for enactment.

I lay down the scroll and looked at them all,
Bewildered, amazed, and uncertain.

How could a tradesman be so versatile,
Unraveling divine revelation! CHORUS.

Today, in your midst, this text is fulfilled
Embracing a prophetic vision.
I wish I was not the one chosen so,
But I can't abdicate the decision. CHORUS.

It seemed like too much for the leaders to take,
A threat to their status and power.
The prophets of yore rejected as well,
I had to acknowledge my hour. CHORUS.

Their voices rang loud with anger and rage,
And they shuffled me down to the cliff.
While wrangling broke out in the disparate mob,
I made an escape rather swift. CHORUS.

I knew this rejection would frequently rise,
Every time I promoted the new.
And I knew what 'twould cost to honor the dream,
The New Reign of God to pursue! CHORUS.

4. Questioning Religion in the Temple

I will never forget the first time I went
To the temple of God in the city.
It stood on that hill, with imperial thrill.
It was frightening and awesome, but pretty.

And they told me at school about rituals and rites,
Set up by divine delegation.
They slaughtered the beasts, spilled blood on their feasts,
A strangely perverse consternation.

My mother had told me that priests ruled the show,
As chosen by wisdom on high.
That strange bunch of men, so concerned with sin,
So addicted to power, I ask why!

At twelve years of age the occasion allowed
To join in a temple debate.
I spoke out my mind, disagreeing with their kind,
The first time I glimpsed my true fate.

My mother went wild at the rumpus I caused,
Disturbing the men in their task.
I could not accept the religion they kept,
It felt false and unreal like a mask.

As they hauled me back home I was lectured at length,
My tongue in respect I should curb.
But deep in my soul I must follow a call,
No matter the ones I disturb.

The Gospels relate that they marveled aloud
At the wisdom and wit I displayed.
A convenient gloss, on quite a big fuss,
When at first my credentials I laid.

5. Nobody Liked an Unmarried Jew

Now a woman might be barren and that's a mighty curse,
And some men join the Essenes, and frankly that's much worse.
And some have been castrated, eunuchs of a sort,
And the few refuse to take a wife, but why they tell us not.
It's puzzling in a culture that respects the law of God.

His siblings all are married, fulfilling full decree,
And his parents did their very best to resolve this jeopardy.
And he isn't shy of women and relates well in discourse,
And presumably is capable of sexual intercourse.
It's puzzling in a culture that respects the law of God.

He seems to have a problem with home life in our land,
And denounces the uniqueness upon which all men stand.
He wants to make the women feel as if they really were
The same as us in everything, as if they never err.
It's puzzling in a culture that respects the law of God.

He sees the family system as a patriarchal lure,
Sustaining all the hierarchies he cannot now endure.
I wonder if he really knows the faith we all believe?
Perhaps, an evil spirit has trapped him to deceive.
It's puzzling in a culture that respects the law of God.

He talks a lot of family, we're sisters, brothers all,
Claiming everyone is equal—a fatalistic flaw!
He can't respect authority as built up in the home.
He has much disturbed his parents and often discord sown.
It's puzzling in a culture that respects the law of God.

The people claim he liberates as foretold in holy scroll,
And some regard him special fulfilling God's own role.
But if the man's not married and will not propagate,
There's no way he could be of God, a social renegade!
It's puzzling in a culture that respects the law of God.

6. Considering My Options

Twinkling stars are gazing down and I cannot get to sleep
My inner soul atroubling, my mental state disturbing.
How am I supposed to do it?
This frightening, awesome call that haunts my passing years!

The other day I fasted as the Rabbi had advised.
My spirit sank deserted, even thoughts became distorted.
How am I supposed to do it?
I heard a tempting voice within, seductive with conceit.

Feed their hungry little bodies and their thirsting minds as well.
The starving mob will follow, and you'll rid them of their sorrow.
How am I supposed to do it?
The hunger of the inner soul is not for bread alone.

Now jump off that steeple high, and land safely on the ground.
Miraculous intervention will surely grab attention.
How am I supposed to do it?
Not with some magic wonders, ingeniously conceived.

Let's go upon this high mountain, earth's kingdoms to review.
Give these people just the honor, a small taste of kingly manor.
How am I supposed to do it?
Not with the false allurements of kingly make-believe!

It was a time of torment, haunting questions from within.
And peace at last unfolded, as heart and soul were grounded.
How am I supposed to do it?
Don't worry, you will do it; just trust in God and risk!

7. Critiquing the Family System

I too loved my family when I was growing up
And the home of my childhood I cherished.
But now as an adult, horizons have changed.
I see the nuances in which we arranged,
The power-games of life were sometimes deranged.
A view so naïve has long perished!

Our family system like an anchor at sea
Kept a tight reins on everyone's movement.
It felt so restrictive with power at its base,
And to question the basics was deemed a disgrace.
And no one would listen to my future trace.
Shattered dreams with no hope of fulfillment.

When I moved out of home the Baptist to join,
My siblings they nearly went frantic.
And I in my turn caused quite an uproar,
When I challenged the Baptist's ascetical lore.
They called me divisive, destructive, and more.
At home there's no room for prophetic!

To me, it was clear that the family scheme
Should be stretched toward a bold new horizon.
Companions together empowering to seek,
A mutual endeavor for both strong and weak,
All sisters and brothers a fresh truth we speak.
No more co-dependent collusion.

I knew this would cause some conflict within,
With parents and siblings and others.
The choices to make will feel like a threat,
Long-sanctioned conditions are now out of date.
With God's reign released, no longer we wait,
But behave all as sisters and brothers.

Embrace then a vision, prophetic and bold,
Declaring this new dispensation.
Companions empowering, all equal and free,
And the boundaries once rigid, no longer can be.
Abandon the structures that support hierarchy;
It's the dawn of a new liberation.

The family system, persisting in time,
Must drastically change and adopt a new rhyme!

Chapter Seven

Empowering the Disempowered: Healing

The essential advantage of a poet is not to have a beautiful world with which to deal; it is to be able to see beneath both beauty and ugliness; to see the boredom and the horror, and the glory. —T. S. ELIOT

The empowering mission of Jesus can be approached from several angles, three of which I highlight in this and subsequent chapters, namely *healing, storytelling,* and *radical inclusiveness.* These are central features of the *companionship of empowerment* (Kingdom of God). Although I treat them separately, they are intimately interlinked, and all three features characterize the upside-down "Kingdom" where the disenfranchised are restored to empowering dignity, their real stories re-echo in parabolic lore, and in the power of Gospel hospitality they know that nobody is excluded from the embrace of God's unconditional love.

The New Reign proclaimed by Jesus is not just for holy people, nor for those with more direct access to spiritual well-being. It is for all those committed to making the world a better place for all God's creatures, human and nonhuman alike. Church and religion have no monopoly over this vision; indeed, at many times in history church and religion seem to militate seriously against this dream for a new world. Nor does it necessarily involve preaching or teaching the tenets of Christian faith. Wherever human endeavor is committed to this ideal, whether by Christians or by atheists, there the companionship of empowerment is flourishing.

Healing is the first strategy of Gospel empowerment for our consideration. The so-called healing miracles are complex stories characterized by three interconnected threads not immediately obvious to the average reader or listener: (1) internalized oppression; (2) systemic disempowerment; (3) displaced spiritualization. In the time of Jesus, to be healed is to be restored to one's social network. Illness is not so much a biomedical matter as it is a social one. In the ancient Mediterranean world, one's state of being was more important than one's ability to function. Healers focused on healing social relationships, in the light of which people could retrieve value and worth and be empowered to live worthwhile lives.[1]

Healing in Gospel terms needs to be distinguished from the medical concept of curing illness or sickness. In the words of one reputable authority, John J. Pilch, "In the entire Bible there is no interest at all in disease, since this concept requires awareness of such things as microscopic viruses and bacteria."[2] We are not dealing with symptoms as understood in contemporary medicine, but with debilitating conditions — paralysis, blindness, sensory dysfunction, depression, severe emotional blocks, psychosomatic illness — brought about by the guilt, helplessness, and hopelessness incurred because of external or internalized oppression.

In some cases, the disability becomes so severe and paranoid that the cultural preoccupation with demon possession completely overwhelms a person or group. The Egyptians held that the body had thirty-six different parts and that every one could be occupied by a demon. It was normal orthodox belief shared by everyone that when the Messiah and time of judgment came, the demons would be destroyed and annihilated. A great deal of projected fantasy — necessary to survive in appalling conditions — is going on here. This is probably the most intransigent disempowerment that Jesus had to confront and rectify.

Healing as exercised by Jesus is not some supernatural power that he alone possessed, but rather a deeper human endowment that we all possess and that God and Jesus wish to call forth in every one of us. In many cases Jesus seems to be invoking in himself and in those he was befriending an altered state of consciousness.[3] At times, this may have involved trance-like behavior, as commonly practiced by shamans and shamanesses, over many thousands of years. Wiebe suggests that Jesus was using a power similar to that employed in hypnotism, a healing methodology known to undo long-term psychosomatic illnesses caused by early life trauma or by the petrifying effects of internalized oppression.[4] In all probability, Jesus was a skilled holistic healer, employing an innate human-divine capacity, which has been subverted in our excessively rational world, and which current holistic health movements are struggling to reclaim.

These observations are not intended in any way to dismiss, or even challenge, the divinity and supernatural power of Jesus. Rather, I am seeking to honor *incarnational empowerment* that seeks to transcend dualisms (e.g., natural v. supernatural), and honor the creativity of God at work primarily in the humanity of Jesus. When we do that we stand a better chance of reclaiming the sacredness within our own humanity and hopefully will work more zealously for the wholesome well-being of every creature in God's creation. For instance, Ched Myers claims that the source of much pain and suffering in the time of Jesus was the brutality of the tax system and the burden of unpaid debts, in the face of which Jesus invoked the liberating role of *forgiveness*.[5] Sometimes the immediate context was that of the forgiveness of debt, and when that burden was lifted, healing and well-being followed in many different spheres of life.

◆ ◆ ◆

The poems of this section embrace the healing work of Jesus across three spheres: internalized bondage, bodily dysfunction, and crippling fear.

Poem 1: We begin with the plight of those in bondage, victims of cruel oppression, which often infiltrated their human psyches, distorting their perceptions, forcing them to project wildly, often with demonic images and disturbing fantasies. In the fall of 2007, news began to percolate that huge numbers of American service personnel returning from the Iraqi war were suffering from psychological trauma. What must it have been like in early Christian times for those under Roman occupation who had none of the resources we can employ today to deal with such trauma?

Poem 2: One of the most vivid portrayals of this oppression is that of Mark 5:1–20, the infamous story of the Gerasene demoniac and the demonizing of the pigs. According to Isaiah 65:4ff., both tombs and swine are ritually unclean. However, purification or expulsion of a demon is not the key issue in this story. Rather as Ched Myers intimates, we are dealing with "exorcism as political repudiation."[6]

The brutal disempowering oppression, from without and within, seems to be the context, with Roman oppression being the primary subject for critique and denunciation. This is reflected in the language used: the word for "herd," *agele,* is usually used to describe not a group of pigs but a band of military recruits. The word for "dismissed" (*epetrepsen*) has distinctive military overtones, as does the word used for "charged" (*ormesen*), suggesting troops rushing into battle.

Some commentators also suggest that we should adopt a symbolic interpretation for the region of the Gerasenes, not far from the city of Tiberias, capital of Herod Antipas. Herod had to coerce Jews to populate the city because it was considered unclean, having been constructed on the site of a graveyard.[7]

Poem 3: This poem is based on the story of the boy possessed by a dumb and deaf spirit (see Mark 9:14–29). In the time of Jesus, and in our time, possession by evil spirits often evokes a type of lurid fascination. We moralize extensively, speculating on what might have led to this awful affliction, wondering when and how the person became possessed in the first place.

The poet wants to consider an alternative possibility: might it not be possible that events throughout a person's lifetime accumulated to a point where the psyche could not hold intact any longer all the inner pain and turmoil and, if you wish, the internalized trauma takes over and renders daily functioning difficult if not impossible? Healing then takes on a different meaning, one that will need to revisit, restore, and redefine many issues that perhaps have never been taken seriously in the first place.

Poem 4: The people were so confused and scared that ironically they could not receive the new freedom that was being offered and, in some cases, began to speculate that Jesus himself was a victim of the demonic. From their dark inner space of utter victimization they sought to scapegoat Jesus, alleging that he too had to be demon-possessed (Mark 3:22–27; Matt. 12:24–29; Luke 11:15–22). Mark Heim offers some valuable insights on the Beelzebub texts.[8]

Poem 5: This poem represents several of the healing miracles recorded in the Gospels. It recalls the well-known story of the man lowered through the roof (Mark 2:3–12), highlighting the strong link between his paralysis and the crippling power of his guilt and shame. Once he knew forgiveness in his heart, he could reclaim the health of his whole person. And this is the juncture where other poems on the theme of forgiveness find their rightful place.

Poem 6: Biblically, forgiveness is strongly connected with the reduction and alleviation of financial debts. It is the right (and duty) of the oppressed to demand forgiveness of the oppressor. At the time of Jesus, forgiveness had to be earned, mainly through the instrumentality of the temple priesthood. To pacify the offended (and angry) God, there were various offerings stipulated in accordance with the nature of the offense. It might be a money offering, but it could also be a bird or animal — except, of course, it had to be the more "purified" versions that were sold in the precincts of the temple itself. According to Herzog, "The only brokers authorized to mediate God's blessings were the priests in the temple. . . . When Jesus announced the forgiveness of sins to the paralytic, he was claiming that God was acting through him as broker to discharge debt even though it meant bypassing the temple system."[9]

Only when the money was handed over and the priests had made the sacrificial offering would God deliver forgiveness. Jesus comes along and, in what must have been among his most outrageous deeds, blatantly dismisses the whole temple strategy. He circumvents the entire thing by claiming that God forgives — fully — and without any bargaining through offerings or sacrifices. Moreover, as Marshall highlights, rabbis of the time taught that people should be prepared to forgive repeated offenses up to three times; it was unreasonable to expect forgiveness on the fourth occasion. For Jesus there must be no limit: seventy times seven (Matt 18:22).[10] The God of unconditional love, preached and proclaimed for many generations, at last broke through to humanity, and what a shock it must have been, but also what a privilege and relief!

Poem 7: Stories like those of the lost coin, the lost sheep, and the lost prodigal (Luke 15:3–32) represent the God of unconditional love, who is not interested in acting punitively (and violently) toward the wayward but always is ready to forgive and welcome them back home.

Poem 8: Next comes the story recorded in Luke 13:10–17 of a woman bent over for eighteen years.[11] What a predicament it must have posed for the righteous patriarchs of the day when a woman was restored to a healed dignity, and from there on could courageously stand up to the forces that previously demeaned and oppressed her.

Poem 9: Similarly, in the story of the man born blind (John 9:1–41) in which his alleged blindness is attributed to a curse caused by his own behavior or that of his parents. In the power of healing he reclaims the empowerment to speak for himself with the daring suggestion that his tormentors should consider becoming disciples of Jesus also. This poem can be used in programs on empowerment.

Poem 10: The healing of the centurion's slave/servant (or son in John's Gospel) stretches various conventional horizons (Matt. 8:5–10; Luke 7:1–10; John 4:46–53). Slaves were property rather than people, and for a Roman centurion to show such love and concern for a slave is remarkable. Jewish/Gentile tensions are also played out in the sense that the Gentile ruler knows he must not invite a Jew to his house. Yet those barriers, whether understood in spatial terms, or as cultural requirements, are all transcended in one of the most vivid examples in the New Testament of the power of distant healing.

The phenomenon of distant healing is being extensively studied in our time.[12] It serves as a reminder, then and now, of how poorly we humans understand our innate God-given powers, and how much healing and mutual empowerment could be made possible simply by becoming more aware. Jesus the healer today would want us to confront the pain and oppression of our world not just as a subject for political or economic resolution, but as a plight that is often exacerbated because more foundational energies are out of sync with creation's own desire for healing and wholeness for all the brokenness that surrounds us.

1. Setting Free from Bondage

Internalized oppression is the greatest curse of all,
So subtle and pernicious in its roots.
It can cripple all the senses and wreck the human soul,
Needing centuries to undo the basic cause.

The people of my culture carried burdens quite complex,
Reinforced from both outside and from within.
And religion left them guilty and badly disempowered,
Even their bodies got ensnarled in the sin.

And when the muted speaker could declare a voice again,
While the listening ear could graciously attend.
The cruel dark pain of blindness was lifted up from sight,
And the maimed knew inner healing on the mend.

And the crippled ones could now dispense of every prop and crutch,
While the leper felt no longer ostracized.
Restoring graced empowerment as God intended so,
Liberated from oppression, they rejoiced.

To this very day they're asking how miracles are done.
They happen all around you in the course of nature's run.
It's people are the problem and the burdens they impose,
Disconnected from the universe where grace and beauty flows.

People still cry out for freedom from many crippling plights,
And yearn for the promise of new birth.
I promised and delivered what everyone desires,
It's up to you to establish it on earth!

2. Demonized by the Legion of Imperialism

What I went through no one will ever understand.
I watched those Roman legions, pompous, loyal, and fierce.
I watched them butcher little children,
While the crimson blood of my loved ones

Flowed down the roadside of my childhood dreams.
They robbed my father's land and left behind
A trail as long as six thousand pounding hoofs.
And eventually they mowed me down,
Not in body — but in mind and spirit,
A tortured soul in the dark recesses of the lake-side caves.

What I went through no one will ever understand.
There were hundreds of us huddled in those tombs,
Premonitions of concentration camps
That would haunt the human spirit for centuries yet to come.
Mid chains and fetters our howling hearts were strained,
While our tortured souls screamed out in utter pity.
We scared the living daylights of man and beast alike.
And dare we venture into the open space
Where gashing sword would often wait our doom.
A legion of the living dead,
The ultimate scapegoats of barbaric Roman rule.

What I went through no one will ever understand.
A fierce fight broke out one day in the asylum of the tombs.
I ran for all dear life not knowing where I was going.
Till I collided with a motley group,
Headed by a messianic freak whose name had echoed in my soul.
I pleaded that he would not torture
My ailing frame already overbrutalized.
And as he prayed aloud my alien spirits to disperse,
My howling screams tore apart the passing clouds,
And scared the swine-herd of a nearby mountain-side,
Plunged into the waters of infested demonology.

What I went through no one will ever understand.
My body rolled and swooned; demented spirits flailed.
My total being collapsed in ghostly stupor,
As if drowning in the lurid waters of the haunting legion.
My mind was dazed for many days to come.
My wasted frame could scarcely feel the loving, caring touch
Of Magdalene, Peter — and the rest I can't recall.
Except, of course, the Nazarene!

And him, I can't forget—and never will.
Those loving tear-filled eyes, piercing the darkness of my soul,
To ignite just one small flame, a touch of tender hope.

What I went through no one will ever understand,
Except, of course, the ones who still endure
The cruel torture of Pol Pot, Rwanda, and Darfur.
The brutal empire still prevails, and legions roam
With the fierce sword of the bullet and the bomb.
We don't seem to have learned much from the atrocities of history.
Perhaps, we need another swine-herd
To submerge the violent urges of the human soul,
And bring a lasting peace to the millions,
Still entombed in the brutal darkness of modern civilization.

3. Possession Is a Story, Not a Satanic Takeover!

For me, it was an uphill battle from the start.
A slow and painful journey through the birth-canal of life,
My little body straining amid the gasping breaths,
Trying to make it through—amid the struggles and the strife.
A signal and a symbol of what was yet to come!

An uphill battle from the start:
My childhood dreams, demented with nightmares so perverse.
I wish I could forget but somehow never managed it.
Why me? I often asked, afflicted with this curse.
And no one there to talk the whole thing through!

An uphill battle from the start: (However)
I was not born deaf and mute—too literal a fact,
Nature's compensation for the cauldron deep inside.
An asylum of the spirits, a noisy one at that,
And seeking that attention to which I could not respond.

An uphill battle from the start:
My childhood trauma mutated into a bruised and tortured psyche.
My people called them evil spirits and said they

Could only be driven out by the power of God Almighty.
But no one listened or tried to understand.

An uphill battle from the start:
Mid wrangling parents demented by poverty and deprivation,
All the money gone on taxes to emperor and temple priesthood.
Our nerves were fraught in perpetual aggravation.
And as far as I could see, religion made things worse.

An uphill battle from the start: (till one day)
At the marketplace I blew a fuse,
And set a frenzied mob at loggerheads,
Scared that an evil spirit had been set loose.
I never saw people so frightened and unsure.

An uphill battle from the start:
Till my dad pleaded with the Galilean!
The final catharsis of many years in agony,
The last hope to demolish a power obscene.
My body cringed, and a volcano erupted in my soul.

An uphill battle from the start:
My body swooned mid frothing mouth and staring eyes,
Tossed and thrown by inner agitation.
So weak and drained they could not even hear my cries,
That sense of being abandoned I often knew before.

An uphill battle from the start:
What really happened, I don't understand, nor does it matter.
My ears unblocked and now my tongue released,
My mind restored from the confusing chatter.
And why do they keep pestering me with voyeuristic gaze?

I think today of those for whom the battle is not won:
Zimbabwe, Burma, Palestine, and many more!
Where spirits still are trapped in evil's prime,
While hope undaunted shines in history's sacred lore.
When will we wake to listen, love, and learn once again!

4. Let's Blame Beelzebub!

Beelzebub or Satan were among his many names
Inhabiting the shadows of possession and their fears.
The spirit of their torture, emaciating pain,
The haunting of their psyche to the point of being insane!

>CHORUS*:*
>*A self-inflicted torture, derangedly obscene,*
>*Abetted by oppression and the rituals so unclean.*
>*The fragile human spirit, so sacred and yet so wise,*
>*Is easily corrupted by a violence deep inside.*

The violence was invented by our own humanity,
And not just the invention of Girard's philosophy.
Perpetuating dominance and competition fierce,
With warfare and barbarity, intense without reprieve. CHORUS.

The coping mind will rescue and liberally contrive
And frame the vicious scapegoat for any peace of mind.
Internalized oppression becomes the deadly plot,
And monsters like Beelzebub have a heyday to concoct. CHORUS.

The people know creation is imbued with spirit-power
And they know the darkened spirit can easily devour.
As internalized oppression leads them further to believe
That 'twill take an evil spirit their possession to relieve. CHORUS.

When I engaged their tortured souls and calmed their frantic glare
I stood accused before them as possessed by Satan's scare.
The strongman in the household they just could not restrict,
With spirit, mind, and body such anguish to inflict. CHORUS.

The healing power of goodness eventually broke through.
It took a great deal longer their fantasies subdue,
And trust the healing Spirit creating ever whole,
And gathered all that's scattered to create enduring hope.

FINAL CHORUS:

The violence of the Spirit is embraced with paradox;
The inner and the outer are an undivided flux.
But the light that shines in darkness dispels the final doom,
So all can know the healing love in which the Spirit blooms.

5. Paralyzed by Guilt

Mid all the vivid detail they lowered him from the roof,
A man whose heart was paralyzed with guilt.
Their sheer determination, their faith in little doubt,
Had heard the healing stories from neighbors all around.
Against all odds their hope is solid built.

And Jesus recognizes the fervor of their faith,
No barrier too great to be undone.
"Your sins are all forgiven, whatever be your past,
And your bondage is unraveled, so freshly rise aghast.
Pick up your mat, and walk into the sun."

But there always are the spoil-sports, suspicious to the core,
Choked up in righteous judgment to the quick.
"He cannot do what only God can do through special means,
What only priests have power to do within the temple scenes."
Little wonder all the people are so sick!

With authority he spoke to them, the sins he will forgive,
For those who trust, their woundedness is healed.
But those locked into righteousness suffer the most of all,
Deluded in their arrogance, a sad plight do befall.
The grace that flows for healing gets congealed.

Then, be wary of the preacher whose wrath is full of guilt,
Whose rhetoric can grossly undermine.
For Jesus is not interested in guilt, or shame or sin.
He only wants the wholeness that comes from deep within.
So, let healing and new life upon all shine.

6. Forgiveness in a New Dispensation

The many temple festivals provided ample space
To set things right with God above and all the sins defaced.
Their sacrifices offering,
Along with so much suffering,
Would surely win forgiveness from the judging God on High.

Now it was a mighty business for the temple priestly caste.
They organized the offerings and did the pleading best.
They alone could please the mighty,
For the humans who were naughty,
They had quite a reputation, this clerical elite.

And along comes revolution as the Nazarene steps forth.
"Your sins are all forgiven," he declared without retort.
Adding injury to insult,
With no mention of an indult,
He rattled the foundations of the clerics' holy power.

You're loved without condition, and forgiven through and through,
And whoever holds you grudgingly, you must forgive them too.
Only God we thought could do it,
When the clerics mediated,
But now the sinner and the saint must forge a new alliance.

Of all the new dimensions, God's Reign on earth reframes
This by far is the most awesome, and the freedom it entails.
No more room for guilty verdict,
For compassion's now the edict.
In the reckless Reign of Jesus, everyone is welcomed home.

7. Lost but Always Forgiven!

Imagine the farmer and the sheep that he lost;
He'll search high and low no matter the cost.
And bind up the wounds incurred by neglect,
And welcome back home both sinner and wreck.
The day for the guilt trips is over!

Imagine a woman in diligent search
For the coin that she lost though it's of little worth.
The neighbors announce the joy of her find,
God's mercy and love leave no one behind.
The day for the guilt trips is over.

Imagine a son who roamed far from home,
So lost and forlorn amid slaves he would roam.
And the shocking surprise of a welcome so grand,
Despite his betrayal of homestead and land.
The day for the guilt trips is over.

And why did we cherish a culture of shame
With Jesus atoning to take on our blame?
It's not in the Gospels which always declare
That sinners are welcome, forgiven with care.
The day for the guilt trips is over.

The punitive God we have known for too long
Is a human projection of the righteous gone wrong.
The healing and love all the Gospels proclaim,
Forgiveness abundant in God's holy name.
The day for the guilt trips is over.

8. Standing Up Straight!

They thought 'twas the spirits inflicted her pain
With posture distorted she moved with great strain.
Bent over by burden for eighteen long years,
With anguish and struggle, and crippled by fear.
To stand straight again, being a woman in sin,
Was a dream she had never imagined!

And the culture of judgment she could not escape,
Some curse from the past they alleged for her fate.
So crushed in her spirit by a faith quite corrupt,
It took courage defiant to hold her chin up.
To stand straight again, in a culture of sin,
Was a dream she had never imagined.

And Jesus saw through the distortions so false,
A daughter of Abraham, she, too, had her place.
An equal in status to whatever the force,
And he called forth the freedom to dislodge her curse.
To stand straight again, in spite of her sin,
Was a dream she had never imagined.

The Spirit of life and the Spirit that heals,
Is the first touch of God to free and release.
The forces that bind through shame, guilt, and fear,
Will never outdo God's freedom so clear.
To stand straight again, and outgrow her sin,
Was a dream she had never imagined.

But the synagogue boss with his righteous acclaim,
Felt his power undermined by this freedom regained.
And a Sabbath good deed, it angered his soul,
While, in fact, he's annoyed by a woman made whole.
To stand straight again, in spite of her sin,
Was a dream that HE never imagined.

When a woman stands straight with truth in her eye,
She poses a threat to all forces on high.
Subdued they would keep her — she should know her place,
But the New Reign of God has drawn a fresh trace.
To stand straight again, released of her sin,
Is a dream for us all to imagine.

She stands in her place, her body aglow.
She raises her voice with the wisdom to know
That freedom begets a new option to grow,
With oppression declared to rule us no more.
To stand straight again, oppression upend,
Is the task for us all to imagine.

9. Let Bartimaeus Speak for Himself!

"Shut up you blinded beggar, you have no right to speak;
you distract the Holy Master in his work."
"Of course, he has a right to speak, and what gives you the right—
to marginate a person just lacking in his sight?"
And anyhow, he's old enough to speak now for himself!

"It might have been his parents that caused him to be blind,
their failure to observe the law and worship God on High."
"How sure you are, you hypocrites—as if you could comprehend
The ways of God with humankind your theories can't defend."
And, anyhow, he's old enough to speak now for himself!

"We think he's just pretending as he gropes about the place,
and probably can't see too very far."
"You're wrong again, you hypocrites, his eyes are open wide,
While you remain deluded of vision deep inside."
And anyhow, he's old enough to speak now for himself!

"So tell us, you're his parents, was he born blind like this?
That being the case, we take it that something's now amiss."
"From early years of childhood he could not see a thing,
but now he sees and praise be God for liberating him."
And anyhow, he's old enough to speak now for himself!

"So, tell us what he did to you, all that messing with the clay,
while breaking all the holy laws upon this Sabbath day?"
"I simply know I once was blind but now the day is clear.
No longer co-dependent, I'm an adult without fear.
And anyhow, I'm old enough to speak now for myself!"

10. The Power of Distant Healing

The official in a panic for a child that's deadly sick,
Beseeching Jesus hurry to redeem.
A desperate situation, a response that must be quick,
And consequences largely unforeseen.

Despite acute anxiety, there's radiating faith,
And healing has potential yet unknown.
As servants rush to break the news of sickness in abate,
The official is a pilgrim coming home.

We call it distant healing, a feature of our age,
Embedded in the faith of ancient time.
Jesus modeling a potential inviting to engage
And heal a broken world for new life.

The energy for healing we scarcely mobilize
And unlock what medics yet must understand.
That healing is a resource we all must realize
And restore our broken world in God's plan.

Chapter Eight

Empowering the Disempowered: Storytelling

Story is far older than the art of science and psychology, and will always be the elder in the equation no matter how much time passes.

—CLARISSA PINKOLA ESTES

When Christians gather to remember and hope, they fundamentally engage in a storytelling process.

—JOHN SHEA

Jesus lived and worked in an oral culture. Wisdom was passed on by word of mouth. Education was done mainly using the medium of storytelling. Proverbs, short pithy sayings, were widely used in daily conversations. And stories of daily life were often blended into great spiritual epics, like the Exodus story from slavery to new freedom. Stories embraced the achievements of the past and offered hope-filled vision for the desired future. Storytelling was the connective tissue around which the whole fabric of life was woven.

The stories told by Jesus are popularly known as parables. Some scholars claim that the parables in the New Testament accurately reflect the *meshalim* of rabbinic literature, a narrative that actively elicits from its audience the application to real-life situations, with themes of praise and blame to the fore. Adolf Julicher, Joachim Jeremias, and C. H. Dodd are frequently quoted authorities on the meaning and interpretative potential of the parables.

Prior to the publication of Julicher's seminal work, *Die Gleichnisreden Jesu,* there was virtual unanimity on the interpretation of parables: allegories used to illustrate Christian truths, equating God or Jesus with the main character (e.g., the king or landlord), and inviting a more God-like response from the rank-and-file (e.g., workers in the vineyard).[1] Already in the Gospel texts themselves, this approach is used as in the parable of the sower (Mark 4:1–9; Matt. 13:1–9; Luke 8:4–8). The different categories of soil are used to describe various levels of holiness or responsiveness in the call to follow God's way.

Julicher's pioneering work shifted the focus from treating the parables as allegories to seeing them as dislocating stories challenging prevailing cultural norms. How did Jesus intend the parables to be heard, in their authentic indigenous context, is an emerging question among exegetes today.[2] In fact, Jesus may have had a different agenda even from that recorded by the evangelists themselves! Were the evangelists already domesticating the dangerously disturbing stories?

Commentators today strive to honor the dislocating power of the parables and the cultural dynamics that the historical Jesus was trying to address and rectify. Equating the prophetic, empowering Jesus with a king or with a landlord has come to be seen as a cultural domestication, a serious betrayal of what Jesus was about, and what Jesus calls us to be about today. What we need to retrieve is the dangerous memory embodied in many of the parables. This is what William Herzog describes as subversive speech, embodying key elements such as shock, surprise, extravagance, and reversal.[3] The inherited conventional world is often turned upside down, particularly the prevailing religious norms and expectations. And the future is left radically open, but with an unambiguous cipher that it has to be different from the inherited past.

Jesus seems to have used parables to dismantle all that was unjust, sinful, and oppressive in the prevailing social and cultural order of his day. In contemporary jargon, he deconstructed in order to reconstruct. He parabolic lore is itself deeply healing, of systems and people alike, but the healing in question is best compared to the drastic surgery sometimes necessary to root out the toxic source of deadly illness.

We tend to interpret the parables with the analytical tools of Greek metaphysics, thus missing the crucial ingredient of the Hebrew visceral spirit, rooted in the ordinariness of the human body, the earth body, and even the cosmic body of all God's creation. Many of the parables are unashamedly human, earthy, and secular. They deal with kitchen-table realities, toiling and reaping in the land, squabbles among workers, wheelers, and dealers trying to twist the system to their own advantage, children playing in the marketplace, the poor struggling to make ends meet. And in all cases — and this is the crucial point — the empowerment of the underclass is the primary goal.

◆ ◆ ◆

The poems of this section are arranged according to their capacity to shock and surprise. In this way we stand the best chance of honoring the subversive soul of Jesus and the call to his followers today to honor this incredibly liberating wisdom.

Poems 1 and 2: I begin with the story of the talents (Matt. 25:14–30; Luke 19:12–28). In the culture of Jesus, a talent was a financial measurement (not a coin or piece of paper money) denoting about fifteen years of earnings for an average person. A person in possession of five talents would be considered a millionaire in today's popular meaning. Now our contemporaries might stand in admiration of a millionaire and feel jealous; in the time of Jesus they would feel a sense of disgust and betrayal. Which brings us to the second crucial point.

The financial climate in the time and culture of Jesus was essentially socialistic, not capitalistic. Anybody accruing interest on money beyond 12.5 percent was deemed to be transgressing, in fact betraying, the core values of the culture. Hence the significance of the Jubilee celebration: every fifty years, all debts were canceled so that everybody could return to what we might call an even and equal playing field.

For centuries we have read this parable — and many others — under the capitalistic rubric of winners vs. losers, admiring the winners and denouncing the losers. That's not what Jesus was about. Infused with paradox and irony, Jesus may have praised the one who buries the talent in the soil (invests it in the land?), unmasks the cruel hypocrisy of the land owner: reaping from where he has not sown and gathering from where he has not scattered. The third person is the prophetic whistleblower who exposes the corruption, and like Jesus himself pays the supreme price.[4]

Poem 3: The parables of the shrewd steward (Luke 16:1–9) and the generous extortionist (Matt 20:1–16) need to be read with similar prophetic imagination as in Herzog.[5] Richard Horsley observes that "in order to protect their minimal subsistence, the always marginal peasants regularly sequestered portions of their crops before the tax collectors arrived or found various ways of sabotaging the exploitative practices of their rulers."[6] To survive a brutal system, there are times in which you must be shrewd, and even devious. Not an easy message for moralists to tolerate!

Poem 4: In the case of the extortionist (Matt. 20:1–16), the phrase "Why are you resentful because I am generous?" is an arrogant convoluted statement to deflect attention from the exploitation of the workers and indeed from all that is wrong in the workers' plight.[7] "Having dispossessed peasants from their land," writes Herzog, "the householder now dispenses a less-than-subsistence wage to the expendables in a cruel mockery of the principle of extension that was to have been the hallmark of the debt code. Any vestige of the debt code has been obliterated by his covetous greed."[8]

John S. Kloppenborg provides a comprehensive overview of this and other vineyard-related parables. Several possible interpretations are noted. The poet, however, favors the view that in its initial context, the parable may have nothing to do with the selective generosity of God.[9] Rather it is, and would have been heard as, a blistering critique of the oppression and victimization of workers, especially under Roman imperialism.

Poem 5: Next comes the story of the king and the wedding (Matt. 22:1–14; Luke 14:16–24). Typically the king is identified as Jesus, an interpretation that is not tenable when the king is depicted as a reckless and brutal manipulator (as in the Matthean version). The story is riddled with violence, and the exposure of such violence would have been a primary concern for the nonviolent Jesus. Unfortunately, as Luise Schottroff notes: "That the kings, property owners and slave-owners represent God has been questioned by very few interpreters of the parables, and it has been repeatedly accepted throughout the flood of interpretations."[10]

Poem 6: We encounter a different type of violence, every bit as brutal but a great deal more subtle, in the story of the wise and foolish virgins (Matt. 25:1–12). This is classical patriarchal rhetoric, with all the evidence of dualistic divide-and-conquer. It is highly unlikely that Jesus ever told this story, embodying the outrageous suggestion that the so-called wise virgins colluded with the oppressive system to exclude and oppress the other women. This is a blatant patriarchal distortion describing a mode of behavior that women would never adopt.[11]

Poem 7: The parable of the good Samaritan (Luke 10:30ff.) is among the most memorable of all the parables, a story however in which one can easily miss the subversive and shocking impact. It demolishes all rules of ritual purity,[12] exposes the priest and levite as absolute hypocrites, and exonerates the hated outsider, the Samaritan, as the hero of the plot. This story should be viewed as chapter 1 in a book of ten chapters — the other nine are over to you and me ("you go and do the same"). The call to inclusive discipleship is unambiguously clear and incisive.

Poem 8: The parable of the woman with the leaven (Matt. 13:33; Luke 13:20–21) serves the very same purpose as the narrative of the good Samaritan. Working with leaven was deemed to be ritually impure and only women were allowed to do it — and always within the house. How shocking — even disgusting — it must have been for the Jewish authorities to hear Jesus compare the companionship of empowerment to a woman working with leaven. This is the liberating power of subversive speech.

Poem 9: According to Reiser, more than 25 percent of the traditional discourse material of Jesus in the synoptic tradition is concerned with the theme of final judgment, and in Matthew's special material it comprises a massive 64 percent.[13] This is complex "apocalyptic" material heavily influenced by the violence and persecution emanating from Roman imperialism in the latter half of the first century of the Christian era.

Despite the fact that simplicity and harsh judgments frequently occur in prophetic speech, the parable of the sheep and the goats (Matt. 25:31–46) was probably never told by Jesus; he would not have resorted to such simplistic and harshly judgmental distinctions. We need to reclaim the insight from John 8:15–16 that it is we who judge ourselves in our commitment (or lack of it) to create a more loving, just, and free world for everybody,[14] a task we fulfill when we feed the hungry, clothe the naked, and visit the sick and imprisoned.

Poem 10: Only after such an overview of the parables can we offer some creative reflections on what is popularly called "the power of the word."

The Greek *Logos* denotes the ordering principle of reason; it is rendered as wisdom in the Old Testament notion of *Sophia,* and translates into the Hebrew *Dabhar* with a root meaning of creative energy that sustains everything in creation.[15]

1. The Parable of the Brutal Landlord (Version One)

Stewing in the wealth he hoarded—yes, he could well afford it!
To spend his time carousing on holidays abroad.
His slaves he trusts with treasure—and to each he gives a measure,
And expects them to multiply the profits rich in lure.

The one begins the trading—while the other adds the gaining!
But the third aborts collusion and whistleblows the game.
And the master away carousing—flaunting money by the thousand,
Returns to check his fortunes and valuate his slaves.

He complements the winner—and castigates the sinner!
Expecting big returns from investments he laid out.
And the slaves that made the fortune—join the master in his mansion,
Now their slavery is co-opted with corruption all around.

And the one that begged to differ — in defiance of all that's bigger!
Thought the money would be better for investing in the land.
To reap without a sowing — and gather without ploughing,
He exposed the brutal landlord and his addiction to consume.

Exposing the deception — the face of raw corruption!
The landlord stands deflated by the wisdom of the weak.
But defeat he won't accept it — and the truth he will deflect it,
While he catapults the prophet to the dungeons of the dark.

In a globalizing culture — we consume just like a vulture!
It's not easy to confront those who worship lurid gain.
So, let's cherish the man of talent — who exposed the truth so valiant,
Offering an alternative to oppressive wealth and greed.

2. The Parable of the Brutal Landlord (Version Two)

The preachers denounce me and moralists trounce me.
They judge me unfaithful, a traitor to power.
A vilified agent and the money I wasted.
I have lived in the shadows of awful repute.

Despite the rejection, no roof nor protection
I stand by my choice the whistle to blow.
I'm anti-corruption and against exploitation.
I don't play the games of financial repute.

It's time for some testing of the Capital system,
The reckless increasing of money to score.
The joy of their master means justice disaster
As the prowlers of profit consume all before.

I waste not nor squander, and my spending I ponder.
I sow where I reap, it's the best I can do.
But the Capital savage must pursue the ravage
And scapegoat the one whose whistle he blew.

The Jesus who spoke it and the church that invoked it
Have failed to connect to the heart of the tale.

To call the subversive and remain decisive
Was the message of Jesus in original lore.

Like wealth that allures us, the story pursues us.
The subversive truth we oft domesticate.
But the New Reign of Jesus marks another excursus
Where the one with the whistle holds a prophetic place.

3. The Wisdom to Act Shrewdly

I'm trying to please the master who keeps demanding more
And I'm trying to please the workers with the favors they implore.
But I can't forget the wife and kids—they are my very own,
While the cousins too beseech me when their money's overdrawn.
Being a steward it is not easy—with demands from every side!

At an unexpected moment the Boss returned home,
Demanding explanations for every sale and loan.
Accusing me of wasting resources in my care,
And threatening my dismissal for not rendering my share.
Being a steward it is not easy—with demands from every side!

The thought of my dismissal sent shivers up my spine.
Condemned to dig or begging sent aches across my groin.
'Neath the pressure of the moment I thought of one way out;
I'll bribe the ones who me have bribed and play a clever clout.
Being a steward it is not easy—with demands from every side.

I called some trusted debtors and reduced the debt at port,
To win their hand of friendship and cushion their support.
Explaining the predicament to swindlers like myself,
I engineered some leverage with options yet to delve!
Being a steward it is not easy—with demands from every side.

Once more the Boss came through the door, I felt my spirits sink.
Surrounded by the swindlers, I could not even think.
He saw right through my strategy, the writing on the wall.
The cruelest blow of fortune, on any steward befall.
Being a steward it is not easy—with demands from every side.

He sat me down in private and stared into my eyes.
He listed all my weaknesses, but said he'd compromise.
He then praised my astuteness and the deeds I swindled well.
And one more chance he gave me — such relief I cannot tell.
Being a steward it is not easy — with demands from every side.

To survive a brutal system, you must learn to be shrewd,
At times you may be devious but never must be cruel.
Although he never told me, I glimpsed the Boss's eye,
In me he saw his very self — a truth he can't deny.
Being a steward it is not easy — with demands from every side.

When you cannot beat the system, you'd better circumvent
And use imagination to temper your dissent.
But never lose compassion, and tolerate the weak
In God's New Reign, there's room for all,
Remember who filled the banquet hall!
Survivors like me despite my repute
Saved by the grace of subversive truth.

Long before they composed "Amazing Grace"
I was rescued once by a strange embrace!

4. The Generous Extortionist

The money he promised was not very much,
But at least 'twould keep hunger at bay.
Nor did I expect we would still be at work
Right through to the end of the day.
Nor did any foresee the trick he would play
Exploiting our meager resource.

CHORUS:
"I'll do what I like with what is my own,
My generous spirit you treat with such scorn.
Take what is yours and go!"

Because we complained, we're often denounced
As selfish and greedy beside.

To question the power of a system in place
Yourself you set up to deride.
To destabilize the values supreme
And scorn the rhetoric so cruel: CHORUS

Most sickening of all is the rhetoric's twist,
Depicting a generous crook.
We saw through the bullshit he sought to exploit
Whatever our ultimate luck.
And we tried to maintain a dignified stance
As he ranted imperial spake: CHORUS

Despite all our setbacks and daily despair,
The Gospel still honors our plight.
And our yearning for justice will one day outwit
The ravage who seeks to exploit
Exposing corruption we must never cease,
The truth for our lives we will risk. CHORUS

Although we're the victims who lost once again
And some feel embittered to rue.
Our hunger for justice is strongly enforced
For a freedom we further pursue.
We believe in our hearts a new day will dawn,
God's justice will surely break through. CHORUS

5. The King Who Spoiled the Wedding Feast

Procedures were in place for the king's son to be wed.
And the banquet hall looked elegant amid a sumptuous spread.
But those who were invited
With dignity benighted,
Had other occupations their precious time to tend.

So the king sent out his servants — compel them to attend.
But they beat up the servants and the king did much offend.
There followed a mighty brawl
By a king who slaughtered all.
And razed their very city to the ashes of a heap.

Common sense alone would indicate that the wedding should postpone,
To reconcile the violence and call people to atone.
But kings will see through what is planned,
Make sure they're always in command.
So quickly find some others the banquet hall to fill.

To the byways and highways he humbly had to go
Till the hall was filled by every seat and row.
The king seemed very satisfied
But still pursued his selfish pride,
And once again disrupted the festive accolade.

As if it was an army, the king inspected all;
And those he disapproved of were kicked out from the hall.
A wedding with a difference,
Mid powerful games of malevolence,
Hides many dangerous secrets that justice must expose.

The purpose of the story is ambiguous and true;
The truth that's spoken here to power, we often misconstrue.
But Jesus would not tolerate
No matter how kingly th' estate.
And if the wedding is to celebrate,
The king must shed his power.

6. Let the Foolish Maidens Speak

We're known as the foolish maidens who forgot the extra oil,
And we missed the opportunity to join the bridegroom's wile.
And despite our efforts at late-night shopping,
Seeking oil to keep the lamplights popping,
They closed the door on our faces,
But we live to tell the tale.

Now this fellow called the bridegroom, inured with pomp and power,
He got us into trouble, at an unexpected hour.
We're told he was delayed,
So why should WE be blamed?

Because the rotten system,
Must protect the ruling male.

While bored of all the waiting for the fellow to arrive
We decided to rest our wearied eyes and slumber for awhile.
We work long hours of labor,
Tending home and land and neighbor.
Would you blame us for grabbing a little time
To rest our weary souls!

So we asked the other maidens to help us in our plight.
According to the Gospels, they rejected us with might.
This is patriarchal bullshit
Which women always outwit!
Women would never treat each other
With such heartless disregard.

Long before Paulo Friere's pedagogy of oppressed,
We were victims of a system but refused to acquiesce.
We embrace our righteous anger,
And with courage we will not falter,
While the bridegroom plays his dirty tricks
We expose the shameful truth.

So come on you foolish people, guard the wisdom of the fool.
And speak your truth with courage in the face of all who rule.
Don't collude with your oppression,
And be risky in transgression.
For the feasting in God's Kingdom
Invites us all back home.

Whether virgin wise or foolish
Whether disempowered or rulers.
In the New Reign proclaimed by Jesus,
No one is ever left outside.

7. The Samaritan Who Broke In

The Samaritan people to whom I belong,
My God, how we felt the rejection!
And resented the claim of the Jewish elite,
The gift of God's special protection
And the curse of exclusion that labeled us all,
Unclean and impure through and through.
I would never accept oppression so cruel
I do all in power to reverse it.

One day as I traveled 'long Jericho's road
A treacherous plight I encountered.
The sight of a man so battered and bruised
Mid the blood of the ritually wounded.
I don't give a damn what religion he is
Nor judge him by any externals.
I would never accept oppression so cruel.
I do all in my power to reverse it.

He told me of people who coldly passed by,
Including the priest and the levite.
And he felt the rejection, a wounding so deep,
So callous and cold in their respite.
So eager to follow the code of their faith
And laws to be pure before God.
I would never accept oppression so cruel.
I do all in my power to reverse it.

And some passing by looked toward him askance
And quizzed him about his religion.
Did he fast and pray—and do so each day—
And obey all God's laws with contrition?
How cruel can we be to treat one like this
While the wounds in his body still fester?
I would never accept oppression so cruel
I do all in my power to reverse it.

On the way to the doctor I met a young man
With a heart full of hope and compassion.
And he, too, had witnessed what I had perceived
A religion too legal to sanction.
I became his disciple to seek a new way,
A New Reign of love and inclusion.
I will never accept oppression so cruel.
I do all in my power to reverse it.

8. The Woman with the Leaven

I have leavened the flour for many a year,
The secret of wonderful baking.
And the smile in those eyes of the children well fed,
At the family table partaking.

But the clergy declare me unclean in my task,
I can only bake bread in my home.
And when I'm preparing the sift and the mold,
My hands over others can't roam.

Because I'm quite skilled at baking the bread,
I guess I'm intelligent too.
And those laws of religion that deem me unclean
Are perniciously false through and through.

And what a delight to know that my skill
Is an icon of God's Reign on earth.
Yes, bread I'll provide the masses to feed
And especially the hungry of heart.

And those who condemn me in purity's name
Some day might grow up and mature.
For the inclusive table of God's reign on earth
Welcomes everyone—clean or impure!

9. Judging the Sheep and the Goats

There are many things in Matthew with which I disagree
Often making me more Jewish than I was.
And that final scene of judgment day,
With the Son of Man in royal display,
Is replete with the distortions that belong to kingly power.

I don't agree with sheep and goats at loggerheads' divide.
For both of them I cherish as unique.
Those binary divisions, they tend to miss the mark,
Carving up existence so clinical and stark,
The kingly way of doing it for absolute control.

And this business of a judgment day for God to judge us all,
You'll wait in vain to see it come about.
In my resurrected presence, with you I fully stand.
I won't come back again to judge, so now please understand
That you pass the judgment on yourselves by the very way you live.

Matthew got it right in calling us to bring daily food and drink,
Hospitality and clothing the deprived.
And find the time and loving care the prisoner to befriend,
And all who suffer sickness you duly must attend.
Then the judging hand of God rests by your side.

And if you fail to care for me in basic daily need,
And lead your life playing out the games of power.
God's Reign of love and justice, you badly do neglect,
Your happiness upon the earth you duly disaffect.
You've judged yourself as alien in this life and the next.

But always leave the loophole for forgiveness to complete
What humans in their weakness fail to do.
An earthly king can keep apart the ones who win and lose,
But God's abundant wisdom has other ways to choose.
Judge not, and you will not be judged yourselves!

10. Acclaiming the Word

Proclaimed as a preacher and famed as a teacher,
No wonder I'm modeled in clerical bind.
There's power in the preaching and control in the teaching,
Quite different, alas, from what I had in mind.

The stories I told them, conversing long with them,
We oft sat at table for many an hour.
With healing for freedom from illness's great burden.
In a ministry seeking the grace to empower.

The word can be heady, cut off from the body,
And sometimes the rhetoric can cripple the soul.
While stories in action, empower us to sanction
The reign of empowerment where all are made whole.

Engaging the adult, away from the pulpit,
A different dynamic I seek to connect.
Beyond co-dependence, and oft childish nonsense,
The Gospel's for adults with mutual respect.

Beware of the teacher and loud-mouthed preacher,
Usurping the Word for pomp and for power.
Abusing the Gospel, with all of the hard-sell,
Leaving people infantile in a game of devour.

So the word I'm proclaiming and the truth that I'm naming
Requires more than preacher or teacher can give.
Empower for relating, and promote justice-making,
An alternative wisdom we need to retrieve.

Chapter Nine

Empowering the Disempowered: Radical Inclusiveness

The poetic character lives in gusto; poetry should surprise by a fine excess and not by singularity.
　　　　　　　　　　　　　　　　　　　　　　　— JOHN KEATS

The companionship of empowerment declares a new dispensation devoid of all the categories and distinctions of the patriarchal worldview. There are no hierarchies and no sacred enclaves. There are no class distinctions and no room for religious superiority. Love is unconditional and hospitality sets no limits. No one is to left outside anymore; everyone is in now. Gospel commensality provides the clearest and most provocative endorsement of this radical breakthrough.[1]

Jewish law and protocol, particularly the Levitical purity codes, stated very clearly who could, and could not, come to the common table; for instance a woman menstruating always had to eat on her own. Social etiquette and religious norm were wrapped up as one. Boundaries of inner and outer, pure and impure, were crystal clear, strongly enforced, and severely punishable in case of transgression. On this score Jesus is undoubtedly transgressing sacred laws and regulations and seems to have been doing so quite deliberately.

For Jesus, this dangerously subversive stance seems to have involved the dissolution of all dualisms and the creation of dynamic partnerships across all the barriers that previously separated and divided people. In the words of Spencer, "Dynamic prophets like John have no greater claim on the Kingdom than pathetic prostitutes."[2] And nowhere is this inclusiveness so obvious as in the practice of table-fellowship.

To the common table Jesus brought everybody, irrespective of rank or lifestyle. Prostitutes, tax-collectors, sinners, the rabble of every sphere were fully and unambiguously included. Indeed, it was the rejects of the prevailing systems who seem to have had the primary right to be at table with Jesus; this is a serious contravention of the prevailing protocol. With good reason, Robert J. Karris can assert categorically: "Jesus was crucified because of how he ate."[3]

97

When first named, "radical inclusiveness" evokes a sense of acceptance, warmth, love, healing, and happiness. All the nice things in life! It takes on quite a different flavor in the pungent line from the Sermon on the Mount: "Love your enemies" (Matt. 5:44). Yes, even our enemies have to be embraced — and fully included. To that extent, we must include and embrace even the most obnoxious characters in the Gospel narratives: Judas, Pilate, Herod. Not merely are we required to include them in terms of the words uttered from the cross: "Father forgive them for they know not what they do" (Luke 23:34); more importantly, love for one's enemy is empty rhetoric if Judas, Pilate, and Herod cannot be included. Here we forge the link between the radical inclusiveness and the commitment to nonviolence (the topic for our next chapter).

On a first reading, John's Gospel seems to portray something more akin to a hierarchal model, with Jesus frequently alluding to the Father-Son relationship, in a way that seems to reinforce key elements of the brokering arrangement between a senior and a junior, a master and a slave. And echoes of conditionality abound: "If you love me, you will keep my commandments" (John 14:15). Is this view reconcilable with that of the Synoptic Gospels?

For many years now, scholars have emphasized the symbolic nature of John's Gospel and the need to opt for the symbolic reading over and above a literal one. Lee is one of several commentators who highlight the priority and complexity of the symbolism in John's Gospel.[4] Writing possibly as late as 100 C.E., the author of John's Gospel seems to have been influenced by the gradual institutionalization of the Christian message, with the progressive adoption of patriarchal language and hierarchical structures. Whatever precisely the author intended, we can and must engage John's Gospel in a way that safeguards the radical inclusiveness as a crucial element in the companionship of empowerment. Poem 4 attempts that integration focusing on the "I am" sayings, so distinctive to the Johannine corpus.

◆ ◆ ◆

The poems of this section seek to express afresh how Jesus activated and fostered this new empowerment of mutuality through calling forth confidence in those disheartened by brutal systems, healing the hurts accumulated mainly because of social and political oppression, prophetically unmasking the systems that exclude and disempower, and calling religion itself to a more transparent accountability.

Poem 1: In the light of so many Gospel allusions to table fellowship, characterized consistently by radical inclusiveness, there is an urgent need to reassess the conventional understanding of that one meal called the Last Supper with the prevailing conviction that only the twelve apostles were present. In the words of Daniel G. Groody: "Thus the Last Supper does not stand in splendid isolation. It is quite literally the 'last' of a whole series of meals symbolizing the final feast in the Kingdom."[5] We must also assume from the Gospel evidence that Jesus used those occasions to empower people in their struggles and oppression, and particularly in the face of the exclusion and social disregard they had to live with each day.

Poem 2: Many of the followers and, especially it seems, the twelve, struggled at great length to make sense of Jesus, his life, and his mission (see Mark 8:14–21; Matt. 16:5ff.). Their tenacious grip on the fact that he was a king, should behave and act like a king, and by implication empower them with something of that sense of kingly power and might, seems to have been an enormous stumbling block for them. Jesus goes to great lengths to help them see the real mission, radical service in the task of the companionship of empowerment. Did they get it? Did they get the alternative nourishing power of the inclusive table? Perhaps to some extent! The full impact seems to have eluded them.

Poem 3: We begin with the uncompromising words from the Sermon on the Mount: "Love your enemies" (Matt. 5:44). According to the Jewish scholar Solomon Schimmel, the Christian Gospels take forgiveness to a level that even the most liberal strands of Judaism would have difficulty accepting. Total, unconditional forgiveness sounds like justice is being compromised.[6]

Obviously Jesus did not intend to compromise justice. Something much more subtle is being evoked, namely, the need to engage the dark shadow that belongs to every living system, personal and collective alike. Walter Wink describes it vividly:

> We cannot come to terms with our shadow except through our enemy, for we have no better access to those unacceptable parts of ourselves that need redeeming than through the mirror that our enemies hold up to us. This, then, is another more intimate reason for loving our enemies: we are dependent on our enemies for our very individuation. We cannot be whole people without them.[7]

This encounter through which unconditional forgiveness is mediated has a power all to itself that no rational philosophy can comprehend or explain. It so shocks the entrenched position of the other that anything is possible thereafter.

Poem 4: The portrayal of Jesus in John's Gospel is significantly different from that of the Synoptics. In John we confront a very self-confident Jesus, keenly aware of and committed to the broker arrangement between patriarchal father and son. It is also a Jesus who keeps the camera intently focused on himself: I am the bread of life (John 6:35). I am the light of the world (John 8:12). I am the vine (John 15:5). He alone is the way, the truth, and the life!

Projections abound in this Gospel, and the focus on radical inclusiveness is in danger of being compromised. We learn more about the author than about Jesus. Earthly kingship with its clear chain of command from the top down seems to be the unquestioned foundation. And the divinity of Jesus rather than the humanity always takes precedence. The notion of the companionship of empowerment fades into the background. Instead, the foreground belongs to the heroic individual Jesus, whose exalted divine status is the primary power to which all must be subject.

Yet few commentators speak negatively of John's Gospel, and for many it provides deeper insight into the reality of Jesus. In Christian spirituality it is a favored Gospel for prayer, meditation, and spiritual growth. Its entire tenor feeds strongly into individual holiness. Something of this long spiritual resourcefulness can be retained, but surely scholars must eventually face the task of realigning John's Gospel in the direction of the Synoptics, particularly with a view to safeguarding the priority of the companionship of empowerment. This can readily be done by adjusting many of the statements suggesting personal power and revisioning them as statements of empowerment. Poem 4 attempts this reformulation of the "I am" sayings.

Poem 5: From the Hebrew Scriptures it was very clear how one should exercise inclusiveness in terms of daily living. You must adopt as your neighbor, as your trusted confidant, only the one who abides by the rules and expectations of the formal religious culture. The neighbor is the insider who knows his place and keeps it. Those who do not abide by the laws, especially the purity code, are suspect and not ones with whom you should keep company. And you most certainly do not bring them to the table of shared food and companionship; when it came to food regulations, the distinction between the insiders and the outsiders was unambiguously clear.

As we go through the narrative of the Good Samaritan (Luke 10:29–37), all the scaffolding around the concept of the true neighbor gradually disintegrates— until in the end, there are no barriers nor boundaries. It is not a case of gradual adjustments or piecemeal reform. It is total demolition! There are no guiding landmarks left except that of unconditional love: everyone is your neighbor! And if there is to be any preferential treatment it is not for the holy and virtuous, but for those condemned to be the nobodies, the rabble and rejected of the prevailing culture. Neighborliness has been changed forever!

Poem 6: It will take longer to change the inner neighborhood of temple regulation, where only the holy and pure are admitted and the unworthy are kept at a safe distance — a theme powerfully illustrated in the story of the two toll collectors (Luke 18:9–14). The one collects tolls as a functionary of the Roman system while the Pharisee is a retainer in the temple system. The former is perceived to be the one who colludes with the harsh oppressor from without and is therefore shunned, hated, and publicly considered to be unclean, while the latter, shoring up the temple system, is a crucial instrument in maintaining and protecting ritual purity, the basis of so much division and exclusion.[8]

Poem 7: A favorite story among many Christians, the parable of the prodigal ends with a twist full of human vulnerability and passion (see Luke 15:11–32). This is a deeply convincing portrayal of the loyal and faithful one who has never deviated from the expected, the mundane, even from the trivial. The shadow side of course is that part of his inner being feels very needy and is easily hurt. He rarely seeks approval but when he does, it needs to be clear and unambiguous.

Ironically, the wayward son is probably a more rounded person. He has known the ups and downs of life. He has been tried, tested, and purified to handle the trials and troubles of life with great wisdom and resilience. He is a classic example of the statement in Luke 7:47: the one who has been forgiven often loves all the more.

The older son has never moved "outside the box." He has remained in the safe, predictable world which is now turned upside down by the reception granted to the prodigal. The Gospel leads us to believe that the matter with him was not resolved. At the end of the day the companionship of empowerment can win over even the most resistant among us, so let's call on the poet to imagine a different scenario: radical inclusiveness won the day — in the end he went in and joined the celebration!

Poem 8: Welcome, hospitality, and inclusiveness radiate through every line of the Zaccheus story (Luke 19:1–10). Although described as a wealthy taxman, the fact that Zaccheus was a tax collector made him a hated target, and, religiously, he was labeled as ritually unclean — hence the accusation of Jesus going to dine with a sinner.

There is a two-pronged approach to empowerment in this story: Zaccheus empowers himself by climbing the tree to get a glimpse of Jesus. In one sense we can interpret Jesus' empowerment of Zaccheus as a reward for his own initiative at self-empowerment.

Poem 9: The final poem in this chapter highlights beyond all others the radicality of Gospel inclusiveness. There are a few obnoxious characters in the Gospels for which nobody seems to have a good word, and among the most outstanding are various members of the Herodian family alluded to in the Gospels. During the lifetime of Jesus, Herod Antipas (d. after 39 C.E.) was tetrarch of Galilee and Peraea.

He is popularly remembered for his role in the brutal death of John the Baptist. Allegedly, he repudiated his wife, Phasaelis, daughter of Aretas, to marry his niece Herodias, wife of his half-brother Herod Philip, whom she divorced to marry Herod Antipas. This affair gained Herod many enemies, and the vaulting ambitions of Herodias eventually ruined him. She drove him to seek a royal title, and he was banished by Caligula in 39 C.E. Known for his opulent lifestyle and elaborate buildings (for which people were taxed heavily), he was intensely disliked as a Roman governor.

Would Jesus forgive Herod? Would Jesus welcome Herod to the table of radical inclusiveness? "Yes!" must surely be our response. The poet can readily imagine a confused and guilt-ridden Herod on his deathbed, haunted by fantasies of what might have been. Ironically, it is in such liminal moments that grace works strange miracles, and unconditional love can break through against all the odds. Even to Herod, we must not deny this possibility!

1. Celebrating the Gift of Food

You take pleasure in this eating and you never seem to fast,
Disregarding all the rules of diet imparted by our God.
"Why are you all so joyless, why can't you celebrate
The blessed nourishment of earth, adorning every plate,
The abundant life of God upon our earth?"

And we wish you'd wash those hands of yours before you sit at table
And purify your sinful soul, from all the sins of Babel.
"There's nothing wrong with these hands of mine, nor indeed with yours beside.
They're God's delightful handiwork in which I take much pride.
The abundant life of God upon our earth."

And we note you ne'er distinguish impure foods from the rest.
To you they all seem equal, a fact our God resists.
"Wake up you silly people, all food belongs to God,
A blessing loved and cherished from earth's own fertile sod,
The abundant life of God upon our earth."

And why don't you respect our law that certain foods are kept
For sacrifice and ceremony, reserved by temple script.
"To me all food is sacred as in God's due design.
Long before religiosity did so much to malign
The abundant life of God upon our earth."

And when we do invite you to be our special guest
You never take the chosen place arranged at our behest.
"Pomposity and honor, I avoid them when I can,
For in God's eyes we're equal, every woman, child, and man,
The abundant life of God upon our earth."

And the company you keep at table, disgusting in extreme,
Even prostitutes and sinners you hold in strange esteem.
"I hold everybody equal, regardless of their state,
For love that's unconditional will always gratiate—
The abundant life of God upon our earth."

Our custom is that certain meals are only male reserve
You insist in bringing women, no apology you serve.
"Your genderizing fiction, misogynist and more,
I embrace a just and loving care, inclusive to the core,
The abundant life of God upon our earth."

And we wish you'd learn manners and behave respectably,
You eat just like a glutton, with a brazen sense of glee.
"I sure enjoy the living bread the earth begets each day
And the new wine full of promise will nourish and sustain,
The abundant life of God upon our earth."

2. The Bread of Understanding

Remember the crowds that were hungry for more.
Remember we fed them with the little in store!
There's bread in abundance, creation replete,
Enough for the spirit to meet every need.
Do you get it? Do you still not understand?

We won't feed the people with Pharisaic law
Nor Sadducees neither respond to the call.
The leaven of Herod will fail to sustain,
Corrupted by power, it will promise in vain.
Do you get it? Do you still not understand?

You have one loaf too many but not enough bread;
The people who hunger are fearful with dread.
They won't get assurance from signs up above.
They need liberation, true justice and love.
Do you get it? Do you still not understand?

The need is internal — the spirit is weak,
Externally stretched by the ploys of deceit.
The souls that are hungry need food from within,
With the fortifying power of a different dream.
Do you get it? Do you still not understand?

Long into the night and for many a day
I tried to impart a more discerning way.
But their minds were still lacking in spiritual skill.
One day they might get it — the truth to distil.
The pathway to true understanding!

3. Love Your Enemies

But, Sir, he raped and murdered my little daughter,
My one and only child!
Brutally snatched one afternoon.
Never again will I hold that piercing smile.
And you stand there and tell me that I must forgive!
Forgive, Sir, for what? Please tell me for WHAT?
Yes, my friend, forgive and love your enemy,
For that alone can calm the raging justice of your heart,
And heal the wounded bitterness of soul.
And help restore a cruel world,
Where reconciliation might begin to flow!

But, Sir, they persecuted my tribe for aeons past,
Butchered and decapitated!
Ravaged and robbed our land,
Treating us like animals for the slaughter.
And you stand there and tell us we must forgive.
Forgive, Sir, for what? Please tell me for WHAT?
Yes, my friends, forgive, and love your enemy,
Because that's the very power your assailant cannot conquer.
And when the nonviolence in your heart
Refuses to couch 'neath the weight of butchery,
You have disarmed your opponent.

But, Sir, for thirty bitter years I was enslaved,
My land and home were robbed,
And now my ailing frame can scarcely
Muster the energy to curse that bastard's name.
And you stand there and tell me I must forgive!
Forgive, Sir, for what? Please tell me for WHAT?
Yes, my friend, forgive and love your enemy,
For that alone can redeem what time cannot reverse.
And shock the reckless bastard
With the glaring truth of redeeming grace.
And defy the very odds of cruel oppression.

But, Sir, I can't let go of that aching pain so deep within.
The sleepless turbulence of sweet revenge!
It eats away my inner soul,
But gives some reason for facing each awful day.
And you stand there and tell me I must forgive!
Forgive, Sir, for what? Please tell me for WHAT?
Yes, my friend, forgive and love your enemy.
The one you hate within, your shadow self aghast,
Can only be restored from deep inside,
Where the seedlings still in darkness do ferment,
The tender shoots you thought do not exist.

But, Sir, why turn the other cheek,
Or in humiliation walk that other mile?
Or give away even my inner cloak.

I'm sick and tired of being the underdog.
While you stand there and tell me I must forgive!
Forgive, Sir, for what? Please tell me for WHAT?
Yes, my friend, forgive and love your enemy
And turn this crazy violent world upside down,
Where guns and bombs and arms
Can be trampled 'neath the footsteps of justice and liberation.
As the reign of God transforms the incarceration of history,
Peace to the enemies we all must love!

4. I Am and WE Are!

I am the light of the world made new
And together with you, my friends,
We bring the light of enduring liberation,
From all those trapped in slavish concentration.
And radiate the promise that will every heart renew.
Behold I make all things new,
Together, we can do it, me and you!

I am the bread to alleviate their hunger,
And together with you, my friends,
We'll reverse the cruel curse of aching empty bowels,
The petrified hopelessness in which starvation howls.
And release the crushed abundance the wealthy oft accrue,
Behold I make all things new,
Together, we can do it, me and you!

I am the vine and you the branches lush,
And together with you my friends,
We'll inebriate the vineyards of parabolic lore,
And pour out for all to drink what others hoard in store.
Clean drinking water every country to imbue.
Behold I make all things new.
Together, we can do it, me and you!

I am the Good Shepherd attending to the flock.
And together with you my friends,

We'll build communities of love and care,
An open table for everyone to share,
With justice to the fore in everything we do.
Behold I make all things new.
Together, we can do it, me and you!

I am the way to truth and life,
And together with you my friends,
We'll level out the shoddy pathways of a broken world
To reconcile and heal the many hearts so troubled.
Transcending what divides us, together we'll construe.
Behold I make all things new.
Together, we can do it, me and you!

I am the Resurrection for new life,
And together with you my friends,
Our earth will rise again beyond the shackles and the pain
Of human's crude pursuit of selfish greed and gain.
Cosmic justice in our planet we'll pursue.
Behold I make all things new.
Together, we can do it, me and you!

5. Who Is My Neighbor?

It seemed like a reasonable question to ask
And would help me determine if true to his task
He taught the whole truth in tradition's respect
And our holy prescriptions he would not neglect.
A quote from the Scriptures I hoped he would cite.
Instead came a story I felt somewhat trite,
The priest and the levite we highly revere
Depicted as demons who failed to relieve.
And a guy from Samaria is hailed as heroic.
At first I did wonder if 'twas all a sick joke.
Am I, too, expected a neighbor like this,
Disgracing my culture and religion dismiss?
We can't just include all the rabble and louts;

We must be selective and uphold holy rules.
We can't just be neighbors, all equal and free.
That's not our tradition nor Moses' decree.
That bastard disturbed me and confused me no end.
He keeps telling stories, my people offend.
To suggest that Samaritans and Jews should be one
Is an insult to God and the faith we've hard won.
I think I'll report him, he's a threat to our State
And has no time at all for the rules of our faith.

6. The Parable of the Two Toll Collectors

One stands in the nave of the temple adorned
Securing his tithes, with prayer he's reformed.
The checklist is long, but he has done well,
And the sinners he sees are all pitched down to hell.
The toll for the temple is safe and secure,
Mid folks like himself who are holy and pure.

The other employed by the Roman regime,
Well versed in the skills to swindle and scheme,
Oft grouped with robbers and downright unclean
And hated all round, being greedy and mean.
He stood well apart, staying close to the verge,
He knows he's unworthy, with so much to purge.

The space of the temple, reserved for the best,
The priests and their allies in God they invest,
An offering so sacred, so pure to regain
What the other collector can hope for in vain.
He strikes at the heart, a merciful plea
And echoes an ache for a new liberty.

The priests are disturbed, 'cause inside the door
Stands a figure impure — no right to encore.
Those who are in and those who are out
Stand light years apart as the scriptures do tout.

"So, who brought him here, our space to invade
Is there in our midst a perverse renegade?"

"Yes, I brought him here," a voice echoed clear,
"And I brought him right in to join priest and seer.
Demolish the boundaries that are sanctioned by time,
There's no inner sanctum; there's only new wine.
So the last will be first, and the first will be last."
While the petrified priests stood staring aghast!

7. Dealing with the Older Son

CHORUS:
He's angry and shouting, with frustration mounting,
Resenting the sibling he wish was not there.
You cannot placate him — so love him or hate him,
For the tables are turned in the power of God's Reign.

"Tell me what's all the rumpus, with music so pompous,
While I in the fields have been working all day."
"Your brother is home, mate, who deserted our estate,
And your Dad's thrown a party to welcome him home." CHORUS.

"Come on in and join them, and feast to consign them;
with the fatted calf roasting, it's sumptous all round."
"I won't join that rabble, carousing at table;
Please send for my father, it's him I'll berate." CHORUS.

"Explain to me, Father, or prefer you not rather,
Have you gone insane like the one who betrayed?
He squandered resources from our hard-earned purses,
And you welcome him back with this reckless regard." CHORUS.

"Son, a father is reckless in loving excesses,
For anyone lost — whate'er their repute.
Your brother is safe, son, like you he's my own one,
My own flesh and blood, now both of you are free." CHORUS.

"But for me, Sir, you never did a fuss nor a favor.
I have slaved in those fields from dawn unto dusk.

Not even a young goat, my favors to uphold,
While he gets the calf we reserved for the kill." CHORUS.

"Son, you've always been with me, unique and distinctive.
What I own is all yours to have and to hold.
Resent not your brother, 'cause I and your mother
Are so thrilled that he's back in our family fold." CHORUS.

"The rules are all broken, strange words are being spoken.
That young guy called Jesus has life upside down.
We must all be inclusive—it scares me illusive,
It robs the uniqueness I too long have known." CHORUS.

"My pride it is shattered and my arrogance battered,
I don't have much choice but to join in the feast.
And I hope I can fathom—the meaning and rhythm
That has turned my whole life—just right upside down."

8. Zaccheus, Come Down!

These short little legs I've had from my youth
Embarrass me greatly at times.
If only they'd find some stem-cell research,
To extend my muscles and give them a stretch,
Then I'd feel a great deal more wholesome.

Thank goodness for trees and my skill at the climb;
At least, I can see what is happen'ng.
But now turned forty, and still climbing trees,
No wonder the kids love to taunt me and tease.
There are times I don't feel very wholesome.

On Jericho mall, they had gathered in force,
As rumor said Jesus was passing.
The sycamore tree was my only resort,
To glimpse the renowned whose fame was afoot.
I saw him and I sure did feel wholesome.

But I did not expect he would stop and look up
And he called me by name—how amazing!

"Zaccheus, come down, for we need to converse,
We'll go to your home and your table we'll bless."
I was shocked but I felt very wholesome.

"But, Sir, I'm a taxman, and not worthy that you
come under my roof in this friendship."
He seemed not to care what company I kept;
With the rich he could mix, and with sad ones he wept.
I never had seen one so wholesome.

The game I had played for many a year
I reckoned 'twas time for accounting.
"I'll pay back the debts to those I defraud,
And give half my wealth, the poor to reward."
The price for a New Reign of wholeness.

Down in Jericho mall as they drifted along,
The leaders resentfully cringing.
"He's gone to a house, a sinner in tax,
He has no self-respect and his values are lax."
If only they could become wholesome!

Someday, I still hope they'll invent a breakthrough
For short-legged creatures like me.
But I'll never regret the sycamore tree
Beneath which stood Jesus and beckoned at me.
A homecoming special and wholesome.

9. Herod's Final Ruminations

I wish I could reverse the chronic pathways of those days,
The agonizing outrage injustice now betrays.
This morbid isolation will tear my soul apart,
Even Herodias can't pacify the rancor in my heart.

My forty-seventh birthday, I remember worst of all,
Seduced by dancing Salome, that bitch was my downfall.
With that head upon a platter and the eyes that caught my gaze
Have haunted me with torture the whole length of my days.

And humiliation followed which the Gospels don't narrate.
The guests were all disgusted and abandoned me to fate.
Till none was left but Salome, Herodias, and me.
"Will you take that goddam platter and dump it in the sea?"

She yelled in consternation like a roaring lion of prey
And headed for our bedroom tracing blood-stains all the way.
Connubial extortion as the head rolled round the bed,
While Salome bolted crazy and in darkness from us fled.

Hallucinations haunt me of the other Baptist too.
The one sent here by Pilate his conscience to undo.
I hoped he'd work a miracle, some peace of mind to fetch,
But he simply stood in silence, with a power I could not match.

Pathetically, I mocked him, ashamed of gross defeat,
Another cruel entrapment, with Pilate adding heat.
"You devious little bastard, I won't fall foul for that;
I'm deep enough in stinking blood, so you can have him back."

I dreamed I saw him on a cross, his gazing eyes in mine.
Am I included in those words, deluded and so blind?
"Forgive them for they know not the things they often do."
I wish I heard them long ago, there's so much now to rue!

The bloodstains of the centuries bedeck this pathway dark,
But somewhere down the tunnel I see a lightning spark.
As I chase a passing storm, there's someone chasing me.
"Am I forgiven, too?" I ask — this paradox set free.

Am I forgiven too? Am I forgiven?
Am I . . . Amen!

Chapter Ten

Empowered to Relate Nonviolently

The poetry that roots up, exposes and gets to the heart of injustice then: that's the poetry that hastens peace. It also tends to be the most subversive, the most feared, poetry, the poetry that upsets the comfortable, that asks questions, and demands honesty of both the asker and the listener. —COLIN MORTON

With good reason, Jesus, like many of his contemporaries, could have espoused violence, seeking to overthrow the Roman imperialism which so disempowered his people, their land, and their culture. S. G. F. Brandon has argued persuasively that Jesus did adopt this approach but that the early church domesticated the truth from earliest times.[1]

Jesus was acutely aware of the political forces of his time and culture. Devoid of the later dualism between the political and the religious, in all probability he would have confronted those in governance and challenged them to behave in a more just and empowering way. Disassociating Jesus from political engagement is one of the more serious forms of cultural domestication and evangelical disempowerment.

Walter Wink, the Jesuit priest John Dear, and most recently Terence J. Rynne draw our attention to the preferential option for nonviolent revolution in the life and ministry of Jesus.[2] It is not an easy option, particularly in a patriarchal culture so addicted to violence. The victorious God of the Hebrew Scriptures is often depicted as a violent warrior, mercilessly slaying his enemies in order to gain absolute control; there are six hundred passages of explicit violence in the Hebrew Bible.

Jesus is often described as a nonviolent revolutionary, and the principles of nonviolence widely known in our time are readily seen in his life and ministry:

1. For Gandhi the first principle of nonviolent action is that of noncooperation with everything humiliating; we must never collude with oppression, our own, or that of others.

2. It is a strategy of speaking truth to power, with a view to engaging the other in a deeper dialogue in order to promote mutual empowerment.

3. It regards both the perpetrators and victims of violence to be caught in the same vicious web; it seeks to change injustice rather than people.

4. Nonviolence accepts suffering without retaliation. "In fact, nonviolence seeks out conflict, elicits conflict, even initiates conflict, in order to bring it out into the open and lance its poisonous sores."[3]

5. Nonviolent love does not sink to the level of the hater, and love for the enemy is how we demonstrate love for ourselves. In loving the enemy we come face-to-face with our own internalized oppression; we both need to be healed.

6. Nonviolence believes that the universe is on the side of justice and that violence merely reinforces more violence. Working for justice through non-violent strategies[4] is the surest road to enduring peace and prosperity for people and the earth alike.

The threat of violence, hatred, revenge, etc., ultimately arises from internalized powerlessness. From that inferior position — often subconscious — we seek scapegoats to pacify our internalized sense of victimization. This can happen to individuals or even to nation states.

The nonviolent option strives to speak to the woundedness, the vulnerability of the other — not from a position of superiority, but precisely because one is in touch with one's own vulnerability. Only the vulnerable can walk the pathways of nonviolence. It makes no sense to the millions in our world addicted to power. Consequently, a first challenge facing those committed to nonviolence is to raise awareness of the cruel counterproductive power games that have become so normalized — and are often sanctioned by religion — in the contemporary world.

◆ ◆ ◆

Poem 1: Probably three of the most vivid guidelines for nonviolent living are outlined in the Sermon on the Mount (Matt. 5:38–42): Turn the other cheek; go the extra mile; give away your shirt. As Walter Wink powerfully illustrates, these are three symbolic gestures designed to dislodge the intent of the other, evoking a need to consider alternative — less destructive — means. This is not just a strategy of being one up on the other, or catching people out.[5] The wisdom and wit to be able to behave in this way come from an acquired skill of spiritual discernment, one usually nurtured and sustained over many years. But let's not overspiritualize!

The way of nonviolence may also ensue as resistance to the demeaning forces of poverty, oppression, and victimization.

Poem 2: In his childhood and adolescent years, Jesus may well have practiced the Jewish religion in its native indigenous context. As he grew older, however, things changed, and in the Gospel Jesus openly transcends the legalities and oppressive elements, increasingly pointing people toward the appropriation of a more adult, engaged spirituality.[6] Thomas Sheehan goes a great deal further: "All Jesus did was bring to light in a fresh way what had always been the case but had been forgotten or obscured by religion. His role was simply to end religion."[7]

The history of the Christian religion has been shaped largely by male clerics, with a leading interpretation that favors the superiority, dominance, and violence of patriarchy. Consequently, the more empowering vision adopted by Jesus has been domesticated and subdued. It is that violence to the original message that the poem seeks to address.

Poem 3: As already indicated the subversive Jesus was transfigured into an imperial ruler from a very early stage, thus losing sight of the Jesus who subverted and transcended the oppressive elements in the religion of his day and who clearly wishes Christians to follow this lead. Jesus, the rule-breaker, is the noncompliant catalyst, exposing the sham, and even the violence, that the observance of rules often sustains. In many cases Jesus is not deliberately breaking rules and never opts to be deliberately immoral. Rather he is transcending the observance of such rules that tame and control people in a way that ultimately subverts and undermines their creativity, an outcome that does violence to the human spirit.

Poem 4: The ransacking of the temple (Mark 11:15–18; Matt. 21:20–22; Luke 19:45–48; John 2:13–16), often named the cleansing of the temple, provides insights into the ministry of nonviolence. Malina and Rohrbaugh observe that both temple and kingly palace claim the same source of divine validation and governance. "Just as the king collected taxes for the maintenance of the elites and their institutions, so did the deity [in the temple].[8] It would be hard to overestimate the import of the temple as the center of a redistributive political economy" (78).

Poetically this story lends itself to vivid detail, both humorous and outrageous. However we must not lose sight of the symbolic value. It is not so much an attack on the temple per se — in fact, all the monetary transactions and commercial activities took place in the outer precinct of the temple. We are dealing with another prophetic protest, a denunciation, of those who disempowered people by making religion so sequential on the law and obligation, on a kind of brokering whereby one could access only the love and forgiveness of God to the degree that one could pay for it — often leaving poor people even more impoverished.

Poems 5 and 6 illustrate that deftness of movement and subtleness of challenge that characterize the ministry of nonviolence. If one alienates the oppressor one cannot hope to confront and challenge the oppressive behavior. One has to hold a kind of level ground, while gradually showing up the weakness of the other's position.

Poem 5: The tribute to Caesar passage (Mark 12:13–17; Matt. 22:15–22; Luke 20:20–26) is difficult to situate historically. Jonathan L. Reed claims that in Galilee at the time of Jesus, there was no imperial cult, no royal statues, and Herod Antipas (4–39 C.E.) minted no coins depicting human faces.[9] The Gospel writers are probably reflecting oppressive conditions of a time later than that of the lifetime of Jesus. Nonetheless, we encounter prophetic insight with strong poetic appeal.

According to Ched Myers, this is one of the most abused texts of the Gospels, so subtly and unavoidably political it catches most commentators off guard.[10] "Jesus deftly escapes the political trap by turning the political challenge back upon his opponents, refusing to commit himself unless and until they do" (314). William Herzog argues that the image of Caesar on the coin is the crucial issue here.[11] The coin is minted in the image and likeness of Caesar; it is a symbol of idolatry and blasphemy (so Jesus does not possess one). The people are encouraged to pay back to Caesar in coins, not merely to pay tax, but rather as an act of resistance and defiance, returning the denarius to the blasphemer.

Poem 6: Once again, we encounter a potential conflict in which Jesus is held suspect for not paying taxes (Matt. 17:24–27). All too easily Jesus could be drawn into an acrimonious exchange. He alludes to the concession for local Jewish people who at times can be exempt from tax, but more importantly chooses to spare his energy for the more urgent work of mission. And he conjures up a rather playful solution to the dilemma.

When Jesus informed Peter that he would find a shekel coin in a fish's mouth, most scholars assume some type of symbolic significance to the allusion. On the other hand, there may be a literal significance to this rather anecdotal incident. Apparently, tilapia was, and still is, a popular fish in the Sea of Galilee, where it has been farmed for about twenty-five hundred years. According to Lynda MacDonald, it is the only large fish in the Sea of Galilee that moves around in shoals, and may be the subject of the large catches to which the Gospel writings frequently allude.[12]

Many, if not all, tilapia are known as mouth-brooders. After spawning, the female takes the eggs in her mouth, where they hatch. The fry remain in their mother's mouth for up to fourteen days before they are released. The female does not eat while incubating her eggs or caring for the new fry. They remain near the mother and reenter the mouth when threatened until about three weeks old, thus receiving protection from predators. To prevent their reentering, the tilapia often store waste materials, particularly coins and bottle tops, in their mouth.

Poem 7: Malina and Rohrbaugh provide valuable background information for the disturbing story of the woman accused of adultery (John 8:2–11).[13] Among the dominant males, it was common for heated feuds to arise when marital relations were perceived to be under threat. As a community response, the woman in question is to be killed, with the hope of thus averting further feuding. Since the woman ties two groups together through their prominent males, her sexual relations with another male is an anomaly with regard to this social connection. Her death severs all ties, legal and illegal, and life can go on. Deuteronomy 2:23–24 decrees stoning for a betrothed virgin who had committed adultery; but for an adulterous wife, Leviticus 20:10 and Deuteronomy 22:22 prescribe death without specifying the manner of execution. Later scribal tradition recommended that adulterous wives be strangled.

Amid such social, interpersonal complexities, violence is made to look both normal and necessary. And all too easily the patriarchal control and manipulation is justified and even exonerated. The task of the poet (and the prophet) is to name the seditious nature of such violence and give voice to the one who becomes the victim and scapegoat of barbaric patriarchal power-mongering.

Poem 8: Nonviolence is based on an authority from within, not one dependent on external validation (see Mark 11:27–33; Matt. 21:23–27; Luke 20:1–8). Such authority arises from a place of inner integrity and authentic wholeness. It cannot be accessed nor understood merely on the basis of external codes or expectations. Jesus' response to those challenging his "authority" alerts us to the corruption and inauthenticity that characterize so much power and authority in our time as well.

1. The Option for Nonviolence

An eye for an eye and a tooth for a tooth
In the system of conflict and violence.
It will not create the balance we seek,
Will fail to do justice to strong one or weak.
Instead we must opt for nonviolence.

Those that resist you with the might of being right
Seek to trap you in hostile reaction.
Beware of the lure to collude with their game,
You only empower them by adopting the same.
Instead we must opt for nonviolence.

Those who attack your repute and good name,
Lay bare your weakness in horror and shame.
What comes round will go round, the wise reassure,
'Cause violence will come back to haunt the pursuer.
Instead we must opt for nonviolence.

And when you're compelled one more mile to go
And you feel you are trapped in a bind.
Keep focused and centered on wisdom within,
And do not collude with the oppressor's sin.
Instead we must opt for nonviolence.

And when others do hate you, return not hate;
Even your enemies you need to embrace.
And when others project their stuff on to you,
Internalize not their grievance and rue.
Instead we must opt for nonviolence.

I know it is hard to forgive and forget.
Some carry a life of resentment.
We judge and we grudge and smolder inside,
And unknown to ourselves perpetuate strife.
Instead we must opt for nonviolence.

A new revolution I wish to declare,
Forgiveness the prize and the victory.

When we can forgive, potential set free,
God's grace abounds in true liberty.
And then we can opt for nonviolence.

2. A New Religion?

Being of a Jewish background, they readily assumed,
A true and faithful Jew in every way.
While others claim the purpose
Of my life and my existence,
To reform a religion in decay.

And then there are the Christians who see me quite unique,
The founder of a faith completely new.
And some say being the Christian
Is the one authentic option
In which the Christian faith alone is true.

I hear patriarchal echoes of dividing up the plot,
The Christian story split one thousand ways.
Such sectarian division
I regard with much derision,
With the arrogance and violence it portrays.

I was never that committed to religion and the cult;
The fullness of God's Kingdom was my goal.
A new way for relating,
In a world contemplating,
Empowering all that makes creation whole.

Institutional religion was the last thing on my mind,
And to clericalize the truth I did not want.
Faith communities in transit,
Fluid and flexible in ambit,
Was the living kind of church I would implant.

St. Paul had small communities and that's what I desired,
Dedicated to empowering all around.

The church belongs to people,
Prophetic yet but simple,
At the service of the Kingdom so profound!

3. Jesus, the Rule-Breaker

Disturbing the peace based on norms and rules
With outsiders in and the wise look like fools;
Imperial forces expect full compliance,
And keep well at bay those who opt for defiance.

CHORUS:
But the Rule-Breaker liberates justice,
and conjures up dreams
for alternative schemes
that bring hope for a different future.

Deconstructing the kingship of glory and power
For God reigns supreme even in a spring flower.
The earth-God incarnate, not in regal domain,
But in hearts and in lives seeking justice to gain. CHORUS.

Empowering the masses toward freedom anew,
To the yoke of the slave we no longer subdue.
Proactive as adults, we question the rules,
And break through the forces that brainwash our souls. CHORUS.

In the New Reign of Jesus there's no one outside.
All the barriers gone we embrace with new pride
The painful exclusion imposed for too long,
Must now be demolished in the journey we're on. CHORUS.

Your sins are forgiven, without recompense
Of temple or priesthood, whate'er your offense.
God's love unconditional redeems the whole lot.
You do the same, friend, in this prophetic plot. CHORUS.

We'll heal on the Sabbath whatever the plight
Of sickness or pain in suffering's dark night.

Hard luck on those who are shocked or disturbed,
There's a call to conversion too big to be snubbed. CHORUS.

And the table is open as never before
Diversely embracing and welcoming more.
"He's eating with sinners" they mouth in disgust.
"The first will be last and the last shall be first." CHORUS.

And all foods are pure as gift for the way
And those deemed unclean are now deemed Okay.
We judge not and won't judge by external law,
Embracing what God offers freely to all. CHORUS.

They stood and they stared, confused and irate,
While the poor of the land proclaimed a new fate.
But the powers soon were panicked and had to resort
To the tactics of torture with a cross in their plot.

> FINAL CHORUS:
> *But the Rule-Breaker's vision had rooted.*
> *To conjure up dreams*
> *for alternative schemes*
> *was a hope that could not be subverted.*

4. Ransacking the Temple

My coins were arranged as decreed by the bank,
A brilliant day's taking for business.
But he shook up the table and tumbled the lot
All over the floor while he shouted corrupt.
The look on his face it was fearless.

I just had been butchering a new bunch of lambs
And a few were still waiting for slaughter.
A carcass he pulled right out of my hand
And my knife it went flying through the window beyond.
While the blood spread all over his garment.

The birds for the sacrifice I had arranged
According to price and the value exchanged.

He smashed all the price tags, and pulled down the rack
With the birds defecating in panic attack.
I never had seen such disaster.

I had just burned incense appeasing God's wrath
And proceeded to disrobe of God's holy cloth.
He tumbled the incense on top of my cope,
Extinguished the candles as I did elope.
The darkness and doom of destruction.

We had spent the whole day refining the laws,
Discerning in detail to match human flaws.
He tore up our papers and spilt all the ink
His lack of respect, it made my heart sink.
My God, what a cruel desecration!

He loosened the stalls of animals bound;
They ran wild inside, even on holy ground.
The pigeons were singing on top of their voice,
While the priests were all wailing, a welter of noise.
And I wondered why God did not rescue.

I watched from the street an exodus new;
The beast and the man shared the same gateway through.
And the birds came as well declaring complete
No more class distinctions in temple or street.
I suspected a new revolution.

I watched from a hill as walls tumbled down.
The old dispensation, I grieved in renown.
While a jug of new wine, I saw from afar,
A new liberation, a bright shining star.
It was scary but so full of promise.

I ransacked that temple, declaring an end
To corruption and power and the way we offend.
God's gracious forgiveness and love to empower
Were lost in a system so keen to devour
The hopes and good will of the people.

The temple that lasts adorns our soul
In the cosmos of life and the earth that is whole.
And God's grace is free for all to obtain
When we're fully involved in the Gospel's New Reign.
And we love, as we're loved full of passion!

5. Tribute to Caesar

They used crafty and devious rhetoric.
They would blind you with words by the score.
"You're a teacher who knows holy prudence
And you always keep God to the fore.
Regarding taxation for Caesar,
We oft are unsure what to do.
We need your opinion to guide us,
Lest we act in a way we would rue."

"Cut out all the bullshit and waffle,
Your ploy to entrap I implode.
Get straight to the truth of the matter.
And show me the coin that you hold.
That glaring inscription of Caesar
You carry around to impose.
I've never possessed such an idol;
My taxes I elsewhere dispose.

"So pay back to Caesar what's Caesar's
If you choose to remain in his hold.
But God calls us all to new freedom
Beyond the regime you uphold.
A New Reign of God has invaded
The cult of imperial spake.
And the coins of the new dispensation
Beget other ways to relate."

6. *Tilapia to the Rescue*

Subversiveness is rumbling in the background
And Peter does not know quite what to do.
That singlehearted "yes" hides ambiguity,
With the words of Jesus adding incongruity,
He's left wondering what line he can pursue.

But Jesus modifies the ambiguity,
Not everyone had equal tax to pay.
And he circumvents the traps of legal coding,
Without entering the web of their foreboding,
And moves a resolution into play.

And Peter grabbed the hook familiar to his past,
Instructed for the shekel he should find.
In the mouth of a tilapia some coins are sure to dwell,
Bestowing them on the taxman, anxiety sure to quell.
Let's not offend a system already left behind.

And Peter sat there wondering—he could not comprehend.
Is this what discipleship entails?
You treat the system lightly and play around the fringe,
And waste not precious energy in seeking out revenge.
Building up the Reign of God in other ways.

7. *Staring in Judgment*

Surrounded by a vicious mob, self-righteous to the core.
They knew the law from start to end, convinced that they would score.
Their eyes pierced through her very soul, as if they'd raped her heart.
And she looked bewildered and forlorn mid a prospect grim and stark.

Mid the scapegoat and the scheming, she stood no chance at all.
With the glee of brutal judgment, her fate set to befall.
Till a voice of pregnant justice ripped through their empty spake.
As she shivered in her shaking feet, she glimpsed another fate.

He kept his eyes down to the ground, while doodling in the sand,
In their attempt to get his eyes, deflected by his hand.
The one without a single sin can throw all the stones he like.
Those searing words of bitter truth cut through their glaring sight.

He kept his eyes cast downward, the gaze went deep within.
It undermined their arrogance and exposed their human sin.
They never once could glance his eyes, while departing everyone.
And through the darkness of the hour, a ray of justice shone.

And now the eyes begin to meet, the gaze of healing hope.
Still trembling from her ordeal and the turmoil in her soul.
And she knows she is forgiven, amazing grace breaks through.
As she stares so deep into his eyes, there's nothing left to rue!

And the archetypal sinner has a challenge new in hand,
To confront the one who trapped her, the real idolatrous scamp.
She'll speak the truth to damning power, each woman new to name.
From this day forth she is empowered Gospel justice to proclaim.

8. By What Authority?

We just want to know if you're really of God
And the power that entitles you so!
You behave in a strange, unconventional way,
The purpose of which we don't know.
And you gather around you a motley brigade
Who show little regard for our law.
And the fact that the women regard you so high
Is a sure guarantee you're a flaw.

You question me much — I have one to ask you:
John the Baptist, from God or mankind?
And don't take all day to figure it out
You who think you're so brilliant of mind.
Well, they pondered and thought and knew they were caught
In something that felt like a bind.
And accused me of plotting against holy writ
What to them was so deep and profound.

We don't understand the tricks you compound
When we question you on holy fact.
We expect an answer that's straight to the point
As the laws of our God do enact.
Instead, you tell stories as if you're a child
Entertaining the rabble around.
Would you ever grow up and behave like a man
And abide by the doctrine that's sound?

Yes, stories I tell of the New Reign of God,
A vision you don't understand.
With eyes that can't see and ears that can't hear
And hearts that just don't comprehend.
And what you call authority is flawed at the core
With power and not truth to relate.
But to empower the masses, the reason I came,
My mission has so much at stake.

By their fruits you shall know them, the fruit of the vine,
To liberate empowerment for all humankind.

Chapter Eleven

What Empowering Discipleship Looks Like

A poet's work is to name the unnameable, to point at frauds, to take sides, start arguments. To shape the world, and stop it going to sleep.

— SALMAN RUSHDIE

Some scholars, like the those linked with the Jesus Seminar in the United States,[1] wonder if Jesus actually selected special groups of disciples to carry on his work after his lifetime. In other words, they query the idea of Jesus being an empire-builder like many of his contemporaries.

Even if Jesus did not deliberately choose followers, certain groups gathered around him and followed him in his travels, ministering to Jesus himself and probably to those who came seeking healing and support. In all probability Jesus cherished the love and fidelity of these followers while, at times, challenging and even castigating them for their incredulity or lack of insight (especially the twelve).

Because of the preference given to the twelve in tradition and scholarship, we tend to think of the disciples as hierarchically structured and formally organized, with Jesus as a kind of boss or manager. In all probability the organizational structure was pluralistic (several groups and not just one dominant one), considerably egalitarian (men and women included), multifaceted (incorporating a whole range of people's gifts, including hospitality). And there is a strong possibility that at times the circle of discipleship was chaotic, confused, reactionary, and very unclear on what was transpiring around and among them. Being a disciple would not have been easy.

Contemporary scholarship advocates that we should speak of circles (plural) of discipleship in Jesus' time and not of a single coherent group. Jesus had several bands of followers and not merely the group known as "the twelve."[2] There is also widespread agreement that Jesus chose (that is, invited) certain people to follow him; the Jesus Seminar questions that assumption, understanding it as a form of "empire-building" that would not have been characteristic of Jesus.

The emphasis on the twelve is probably symbolic rather than factual, represent-ing the twelve tribes of Israel and thus serving as a symbol of continuity between the Hebrew faith and the newly emerging Christ sect.[3] That there was an ac-tual group of twelve is supported by modern scholars such as Dunn,[4] who opts for taking the evidence seriously, and draws heavily on an oft-quoted article of John P. Meier.[5] Catholic scholars such as Meier prioritize the twelve above all the other groupings, viewing them as the foundations for the apostolic succession upon which the papacy and priesthood of the church are founded. Other schol-ars emphasize the diversity of the various groups of disciples, and some favor the subverted group led probably by Mary Magdalene (see chapters 12, 13, and 14).

We will probably never surface historical evidence for either the twelve as indi-viduals nor their precise group function in the time of Jesus. Meanwhile, we get important insights into their human characters and the poet can readily embellish their personal portraits. What is most encouraging, and perhaps was also most significant for Jesus, is their sheer humanity, and wonderful mixture, depicting all that is great and fragile in the human condition.

◆ ◆ ◆

Poem 1: Crossan and Reed provide a vivid and disturbing portrayal of collabora-tive ministry in the decades immediately following the death of Jesus.[6] Paul and the woman Thecla seem to have enjoyed total equality in all aspects of Christian min-istry, but already by the mid-century, or shortly thereafter, a violent anti-woman movement arose, violating that collaborative empowering model of discipleship in which both sexes enjoyed not merely equality but a strong sense of egalitarian mutuality. This vouches for the view that Jesus had not one but a range of diverse colleagues who engaged collaboratively in Christian ministry and service at a range of different levels.

Poem 2: Despite the fact that we know little or nothing about the twelve as indi-viduals, or even as a group, they clearly portray a vivid collage of human diversity, ordinariness, and the transforming power of incarnational grace. If these strange and amazing creatures were special for Jesus, then all of us are special. For the poet, this is what makes them distinctive, not some elite status through which apostolic succession is mediated, but rather their unambiguously radiant humanity in all its fickleness, beauty, and fragility.

Poem 3: According to Madden, Peter's life, like our own, tends to be dictated by a recurring behavior pattern: *pride, fall, rescue, and restoration.*[7] When the going is good Peter is in his element and exhibits those qualities of leadership and empowerment we all so deeply admire. It's when things are going pear-shaped that Peter no longer feels in control of what is happening and we see a very insecure, fearful, and reactionary human being. In the end, it may well have been his stubborn steadfastness that carried him through great suffering and trial to the point of martyrdom.[8] For the poet his greatness is not in the power he represents for apostolic succession, but in his surrender to the amazing grace that can transform even the most dysfunctional lives.

Poem 4: With so many urgent ecological and environmental issues confronting humanity today, Christians often ask: To what extent does the material creation come into the Gospels? Is Jesus interested in the welfare and evolution of creation? Scholars such as Herzog and Horsley declare unambiguously that Jesus very much endorsed the Jewish conviction that the land is God's great covenantal gift to the people, and that this is the background to many of the parables dealing with landowners and workers.[9]

Even if Jesus in his day was very explicitly committed to an earth spirituality (which he probably was), the Gospel writers, under the dualistic Greek influence, would probably not have recorded much about it. We have no way of retrieving what Jesus might have said regarding an earth spirituality. We are on much more authentic grounds by imagining what a contemporary Jesus would have to say on the subject, within the context of the companionship of empowerment. Certainly today Jesus would want us not merely to include the earth in the work of discipleship but also to make it the focus in all the expressions of our Christian life and ministry.

Poem 5: Some contemporary scholars suggest that we should regard the Transfiguration (Mark 9:2–10; Matt. 17:1–9; Luke 9:28–36) as a post-Resurrection story. It contains a great deal of archetypal imagery, and whatever its precise context, clearly it is intended to reassure and encourage the apostles (represented in the three) for the difficult and bewildering times ahead. Perhaps, that still continues to be one of its main functions: to encourage us all as we too strive to be faithful and creative disciples in the companionship of empowerment.

Poem 6: The story of the brothers James and John seeking privileged places in heaven (Mark 10:35–45; Matt. 20:20–28) is another manifestation of the sheer ordinariness of the apostles, preoccupied with their own survival and hoping there would be some extra rewards in it for them. From a life of ordinariness, and perhaps social impoverishment and oppression, they dreamed not only of a better human future but also the exultation of heavenly status.

There is a patriarchal twist to the tale that needs to be challenged forthrightly in all forms of Christian discipleship, namely, the suggestion that the mother is the one who is pushing them for the special status they seek. Such a move portrays her as the guilty one and leaves the males off the hook. This is a classical device of displacing blame and guilt, all too common in patriarchal regimes.

Poem 7: Casting out demons seems to have been a major preoccupation in the time of Jesus, and on a few occasions, some of the disciples seem to resent the fact that others exercised a power of exorcism (Mark 9:38–40). The issue seems to be fraught with possible misunderstanding, including the allegation that Jesus casts out evil spirits because he is himself in the grip of an evil spirit. In the confusion of the times, it is also possible that those of rank-and-file status would jump to this conclusion, possibly requesting Jesus to leave their territory as allegedly happened after the Gerasene episode (recorded in Mark 5:17).

This poem is dedicated to all who are called to the prophetic edge, in recognition of the heavy price they may have to pay in their prophetic discipleship. By embracing the deep pain and struggle of a people, by opening up alternative ways of being, the prophet offers hope and new vision, but at times this is so disturbing of the status quo that it evokes a negative reaction from the very people who are likely to benefit most from the new empowerment.

Poem 8: The subject of this poem is Peter's mother-in-law (see Mark 1:29–31; Matt. 8:14–16; Luke 4:38–41), but as Kathy Coffey deftly suggests, there may be another twist to the plot, namely, that Peter's wife had itchy feet and wanted to join the itinerant band of disciples.[10] This may not be as far-fetched as it initially seems. There is some evidence that husband-and-wife couples were among the followers of Jesus;[11] we also see couples active in the early Pauline church.

There is something strangely empowering in the notion of an older woman, sick in bed with fever yet awakened into healing. Through her hospitality and homemaking she empowers the ministry of discipleship and the new life it makes possible for others.

1. Collaborative Discipleship

Blessed are those who came along not knowing what to expect.
Enamored by a holy lure, they just could not reject.
Blessed are those who left behind the things they cherished most
And risking all, embraced a call,
Without quite knowing the cost.

Blessed are those disciples who were never named unique.
Whether numbered in the hundreds or the two plus seventy.
Blessed are those who helped my cause in small and great alike.
In the shaping of God's Reign on earth,
Showed resilience and might.

Blessed are the twelve apostles by the Gospels to the fore,
Modeled on the tribes of Israel held their place in sacred lore.
Although exaggerated, as distinctive from the rest,
Representing what was ordinary,
They did their very best.

Blessed especially the women with gifts exemplary.
It's disgusting how the Gospels ignore them virtually.
Blessed particularly that woman, from Magdala her fame.
She held the group together,
Ever faithful to my name.

I may have had my favorites like Magdalene and John,
But cherished all the others engaged in my mission.
And despite their limitations they together contribute
To the building of the Kingdom,
In fidelity and truth.

2. They Are Known as the Twelve

My name is Andrew from the region of Bethsaida.
I proudly rank among the first he called.
And I led Peter to him and many Greeks enthralled.
I sometimes wondered what 'twas all about,
To follow closely with a heart so full of doubt.

My name is Simon, but better known as rock-like Peter!
I liked the power he offered, the status and the rank,
But the many times we argued made me sound much like a crank.
He floundered me at times with his messianic zest,
And should not have called me Satan in front of all the rest.

My name is James, son of Alphaeus, and lesser of the two.
The drudgery of fishing I was happy to let go,
And elevate my family in ranks of social flow.
At times it was a nightmare, my wits just at an end,
To explain to wife and family who could not comprehend.

My name is Thomas, and I must admit I do not like
The doubting fame I frequently ignite.
The others, too, were often full of doubt,
But I hung in and even to India in the South
I took the Good News and gave my very life.

My name is John, reputed as the son of Thunder.
I sacrificed so much it left me wonder!
So, with the brother I sought a surer grace,
The guarantee hereafter in Heaven's right-hand place,
Especially enamored by his transfigured face.

My name is James, the son of Zebedee,
And like my brother, John, had sought priority.
I know I was mistaken in seeking special favor,
And I hope I compensated by later faithful labor
Till Herod called my final toll in the year of 44.

My name is Bartholomew, or Nathaniel if you wish.
I'm not sure why I followed, I just admired him so.
The hope and joy he offered when people felt so low.
I often felt the lame duck in a mighty enterprise
But tried my best to heal the wounds of many anguished cries.

My name is Matthew, collector of the tax aghast.
What a relief it was to be called beyond that dreary task!
At least I now had friends, though we often disagreed

Not knowing the implications of this messianic creed.
And eventually I wrote it down for ages to recall.

My name is Simon, reputed fan of zealot fame.
For many years, the Roman power I sought to expurgate
Till I realized that armed struggle would never alter fate.
I joined the Jesus movement in the hope I might begin
To activate true freedom, a revolution from within.

My name is Jude, the saint you claim for hopeless fame.
An introvert by nature, the limelight I keep low.
I wash the pots and dishes and watch the daisies grow.
Yet, the seekers all consult me, my wisdom to access.
It seems to help their troubled hearts and drive away distress.

My name is Judas, with haunting memories so wrong.
I loved that guy, believe me so, and really hoped
He would deliver what was promised long ago.
I betrayed him, expecting a miraculous breakthrough.
But it was not to be, a mistake I bitterly do rue.

My name is Jesus, yes, I chose this motley bunch
As God has chosen you—without distinction!
Reserving mission to the twelve, the Gospel does not mention.
Instead they manifest discipleship so real,
The rank and file of daily life, on these I place my seal.

3. That Guy Called Peter

When things were going well and he felt in control,
There was no one as cheerful as Peter.
The power and the glory of getting it right
Boosted all of his hopes to be greater.
To lay down his life for Jesus he would
As long as the cross is not mentioned.
While reaping success he will go any length
As long as his prospects are sanctioned.

The higher one goes the rougher the fall;
Despair can so quickly take over.
The hero collapses and loses the plot,
And acts like a nervous controller.
And when Peter is down, it's really the pits,
And everything looks rather hopeless.
He's easily panicked and becomes insecure
With a past often loaded with remorse.

A script of dependency comes into play
Awaiting the one who will rescue.
And although he has played the game many times
Has not learned the wisdom to undo.
A reminder for all of the strange power of grace
The sinner who knows it abundant.
And for Peter it helps to survive the pace,
Even when all hope's abandoned.

Yes, back he will bounce defying the odds,
And throw his weight into the endeavor.
And despite the mistakes he has often made
He knows God is faithful forever.
In a strange kind of way his faith is sustained
By the failure evoking conversion.
He'll more than survive the hard knocks of life
Unstinting and faithful to mission.

We've all been inspired by the fisherman's lure.
We know his perverse consternation.
And we know all too well his sheer heart of gold
Surviving the harshest ruination.
A leader indeed from the furnace of life
With a shadow no one can elude.
If history had honored this paradox mix
Then Peter would glow as an icon of truth.

It's the power and the glamour invoked in his name
Dishonors his greatness and the truth of his fame.

4. Discipleship and the Care of Creation

The Gospel is an enterprise you carry in your heart,
A grace to share abundantly, a wisdom to impart.
Devoid of the resources we feel we must possess,
The power and wealth of knowledge and elegance of dress,
With mighty words and arguments opponents to impress.
We mouth aloud the Scriptures, conversions by the score.
It leaves me tired and weary,
My heart so sick and dreary,
Pontificating power games I recognize no more.

Co-working with my colleagues in the shantytowns of life,
No money in our purses, bare clothing to survive.
At home with hospitality, we give as we receive,
But the message of true justice, we'll faithfully release.
And when they do denounce us, imprison us as well,
Disciples of nonviolence, our hope they will not quell.
We don't support the empire with the kingly power on high.
There's another dispensation,
At the heart of God's creation
And that's the Reign of God on earth whose time is ever nigh.

Now Matthew tried to tell us that Good News we reserve
For the holy ones of Israel, their treasure to preserve.
There are no sacred enclaves in the Reign of God set free,
Embracing God's creation in mountain, vale, and sea.
To work for right relationships with justice to the fore,
With love and liberation — and true joy to endure.
Embracing with a conscience the earth we're asked to care
Creation's cruel atrocity
Cries out as well for liberty;
The earth we have too long ignored demands a righteous share.

5. The Transfiguration

We're mentioned in the story, but we never had a say,
That strange transfigured moment of our lives.
Another of those meetings in the mountainy recluse,
Discussing all the problems in the missionary use.
And the warning of the troubles up ahead.

Our eyes drooped off in slumber in consciousness so deep,
We were jolted into imagery intense.
An aura white and glistening, with Jesus center-place,
With Moses and Elijah fulfilling empty space,
And a voice saying, "It's my beloved Son."

Well, Peter went hysterical and there's nothing new in that:
Erect some tents of permanence to mark the special spot.
The thrill he hoped forever last,
Allay his doubts and fears so vast.
But the rest of us knew well enough there was more to it than that.

We figure 'twas a special grace to prepare us for the worst.
The glory we all longed for would entail a painful cross.
Listen deeply to the wisdom,
With fortitude and vision.
We were very slow to question what exactly it all meant.

As for Peter and his antics, he took time to quiet down
And reverted to a snoring that shook everything around.
Back to sleep we all returned
Till the dawn's new day unfurled.
Descended from the mountain, to the plains of daily life.

6. Those Self-Important Brothers

"Our parents convinced us we should work very hard
And with fruit to our labors we could reap a reward.
It's nice to know sometimes as we climb up the steps
That it's worth all the effort and we'll have no regrets.

So the mother suggested we come straight to the point
And get it in writing that you'll choose to anoint.
We, two special brothers, be close by your side
And reign in your glory with honor and pride."

"I'm oft asked for favors by many in need
And I try to respond with a dignified heed.
But this request of the brothers is strangely unreal
From those called to serve in the Kingdom's appeal.
You don't know what you're asking, this favor so strange.
I don't grant positions in this heavenly range.
Our mission is service, a sweet bitter cup
Which together we drink till our life's work is done."

"Yes, the cup we can drink as we follow along,
But we'd like to be sure of which rank we belong.
With winners and losers competing so fierce
We need guarantees that our odds will increase."
No wonder the others indignant they felt.
This game of competing does little to help.
It poisons the spirit and sullies the soul
And undermines hope in the desire to be whole.

The brothers reflect what the others felt too,
So widespread the yearning to power and to rule.
But the Gospel of Jesus leads another refrain.
It's in serving the other, our reward we will gain.
We give away life and the future we trust
To One who empowers both the last and the first.
We're servants in mission all the days of our life.
We're servants forever and therein we survive.

7. How Could He Cast It Out?

He's not one of us, so how could he do it
Expelling a demon in your holy name?
He's not one of us, the specially chosen,

Usurping our privilege and robbing our gain.
So stop his marauding on our privileged status,
And stand by the ones that are really your own.

My friends and companions, how long will it take me
To open your eyes to the hope that is new?
The new dispensation of justice and freedom
Includes all God's people and not merely you.
So, relish the gifts that others can bring us.
They too can set free from the bondage of old.

But Master, you told us that we would be special;
The true faith of Israel we always uphold.
And all those outsiders, impure and uncultured,
Are not yet redeemed and your laws they don't hold.
Invoking your name to cast out those demons
Is really for us, the holy and saved.

My friends and companions, you're stuck in false grandeur.
I called you to service, not glory to gain.
No privileged places in this dispensation
But welcome for all who share my new dream.
So, open your hearts, for no one's excluded
And embrace diverse gifts for healing and hope.

Two thousand years later, we're still regulated
By barriers so rigid, both inside and out.
The jealous resentment with violence demented,
The breakthrough to freedom has yet to take place.
Beyond creed and color, let's create a new mural
Where everyone's cherished in a New Reign of peace.

8. Peter's Mother-in-Law

Yes, I got sick and took to the bed,
I think 'twas the worry and strain,
with a daughter at times going insane.
And children caught up in confusion

With their father gone off on a mission.
My husband had died just a few months ago
Moved in with the daughter my spirits being low,
If only I knew
What I would here endure
I'd just have stayed home on my own.

I heard all the rumpus and noise,
The children went wild their father to see,
They climbed on his shoulder and some on his knee.
And all the strange people together they spoke,
I heard my name mentioned as prayer was invoked.
I can never recall such attention received,
Everyone so concerned my pain to relieve.
A stranger's embrace
Like infusion of grace,
I could feel it going right through my body.

Something strange had transpired in the depth of my soul
And I thought I would help out my daughter.
These guests we would somehow look after.
And I wanted the chance to get Peter's attention
And berate the neglect of his wife and his children.
And to try and placate a wife who was eager
To embrace the call as a new Kingdom seeker.
But the eye of the stranger
Had outpaced the arranger,
Telling me all would be well mid the hour of great need.

Something changed in the household that day.
I prayed for the wisdom to do what was right
'Cause my son-in-law, Peter, was not very bright.
I agreed to look after the children with care,
Their mother for mission with Peter to share.
She too was intrigued with the guru who led,
The sick he had healed and the hungry he fed.
Discipleship lured her along,
Her faith became solid and strong.
While I had to learn once more the skill of a mothering hand.

It somehow turned out for the best.
What was happening around me I did not understand.
Both Peter and Lizzy claimed it all of God's plan.
Sometimes crowds in their droves would follow in zeal,
While the priests their resentment they could not conceal.
I sensed a big change was afoot for us all
And I hoped that the end to oppression would call.
A future the children deserve,
With peace and good will in reserve.
And I hope I too did contribute to building God's New Reign on earth.

Chapter Twelve

Empowerment as Women's Liberation

The farthest horizons of our hopes and fears are cobbled by our poems.
— AUDRE LORDE

Courage to be is the key to the revelatory power of the feminist revolution.
— MARY DALY

Women feature frequently in the Gospels — and in the story of Jesus — yet we know little or nothing about most of them. In some cases they are not even named. Frequently their value and virtue are depicted in terms of how well they serve the patriarchal agenda of subservience, passivity, false humility, and service to the needs of leading males. Marcus Borg depicts the disturbing scene:

> A good wife was much appreciated, but women as a group were not thought well of. The synagogue prayer recited at each service included the words: "Blessed art thou, O Lord, who hast not made me a woman." In synagogues women typically were required to sit in a separate section and were not counted in the quorum of ten people needed to hold a prayer meeting. They did not teach the Torah, and as a general rule were not even to be taught the Torah.[1]

For much of Christendom, Gospel women were subdued, maligned, and made invisible. Thanks to more comprehensive approaches to the study of Scripture in the nineteenth and twentieth centuries, a new freedom of thought and more integrity in research allowed the real women to surface. Today we have a growing body of evidence of an egalitarian spirit in early Christian times, what Elisabeth Schüssler Fiorenza calls the discipleship of equals.[2] Kathleen Corley goes a great deal further, suggesting that the foundations for such egalitarianism were already there in the ancient Jewish culture.[3]

John Dominic Crossan notes that Paul's letter to the Romans (written in the
50s) was carried by a woman whose responsibilities would also include reading,
circulating, and explaining the contents to the Roman recipients.[4] In Romans
16:1–15, Paul greets twenty-seven Christians, ten of whom are women; how-
ever, of those singled out for special mention six are men while five are women,
And when Paul uses the word *kopiao,* meaning "to work hard," he uses it of him-
self twice in Galatians 4:11 and 1 Corinthians 15:10, but four times in Romans
applied to women only.

Crossan and Reid cite evidence for the equality of Paul and Thecla in every
aspect of ministry in the early decades of the Christian community, a partnership
that seems to have been undermined already by the middle of the first Christian
century.[5] Finally, Elsa Tamez makes a convincing case that Timothy's anti-women
rhetoric in 1 and 2 Timothy is evidence of a strong leadership role, and possibly a
financial role, of women in the churches of the time.[6]

In the closing decades of the twentieth century a flurry of literature began to
surface, seeking to rehabilitate — in the name of truth and justice — the many
women who contributed to the creation of the early Christian church, both during
and after the life of Jesus.[7] These works broadly agree on the following points:

- Jesus worked zealously for the empowerment of women, and women were
  probably among his most reliable and creative disciples.

- The evidence for women in the Jesus ministry has been seriously subverted and
  in many cases made totally invisible.

- The Gospels hint at women serving mainly in a supportive role, including fi-
  nancial assistance; in all probability they were also involved in preaching and
  healing.

- The patriarchal distrust of women is obvious in the subjugated roles attributed
  to them in the Gospels. Even Luke, who mentions women more frequently
  than others, typically depicts them in obedient submission to leading males.[8]

- Most women in the time of Jesus were homemakers, not educated like men,
  and usually prohibited from financial or legal transactions. However, to func-
  tion effectively as homemakers and land-carers in Palestine of the time, they
  would need to be (as Elizabeth Johnson points out) skillful, robust, confident
  in disposition, and possibly a great deal more articulate than the conventional
  stereotypes suggest.[9] There is also some evidence to show that women of Roman
  aristocratic background enjoyed great freedom and had access to education,
  which may have had an impact by the time of the first Christian century.[10]

◆ ◆ ◆

Poem 1: The poems in this section begin with Mary the Mother of Jesus. This is the archetypal birthing woman, the "Mitochondrial Eve" of contemporary science.[11] She continues the tradition of the Great Mother Goddess and the Sophia woman of the Wisdom literature and is the forerunner of the Black Madonna. Erotic, sensuous, unashamedly embodied, earthy, and cosmic, not only is she a worthy medium for a divine theophany, but she is also a primordial model for all that is beautiful, fruitful, and promising in men and women alike.

   With her opening words, the stage is set for the other liberated and liberating women who adorn the pages of the Gospels. We will probably never fully know the true scale of their contribution.

Poem 2: This poem is based on a provocative passage in Luke's Gospel, 11:27–28, challenging the misogynist tendency to see a woman comprised mainly of breasts and genitals, the reproductive agent highlighted by Aristotle. This is a form of biological reductionism that Jesus clearly denounced along with the innate corrupt sexism well named by the contemporary British sociologist Tamsin Wilton: "The famously erotophobic Marian discourses of female sexuality seem to have reinforced both the notion that sex was not to be spoken of and that women should not find it pleasurable. . . . Women themselves are socialized to regard — even to experience — their dreams and their sexuality as trivial and insignificant. Thus, woman's desire is presented to them as something organized around reproductive matrimonial heterosex."[12]

Poem 3: The anointing story in Luke 7:36–50 is so rich it merits a whole book in its own right. One of the most empowering lines in the story, as noted by scholars such as Culpepper and Reid, is the question posed by Jesus to Simon: "Are you actually capable of seeing who and what this woman is in her core identity?"[13] We need to raise this question for every single woman in the New Testament. When we begin to see afresh, with a discerning contemplative gaze, such may be the new insights that large sections of the Scriptures may need to be revised. According to John 12:3, Mary the sister of Martha is the woman in question but as Bauckham indicates, there is little agreement on who precisely it might be. For the poetic imagination, Mary Magdalene is the more favored candidate.[14]

Poems 4, 5, 6: In these three poems we evidence some amazing self-empowerment by Gospel women:

Poem 4: In the story of the Syrophoenician woman (Mark 7:24–30; Matt. 15:21–28) it looks like Jesus has made an almost unforgivable blunder. He plays the party card, that salvation is only for the Jews, but the Syrophoenician woman will not let him get away with that harsh moralistic exclusion. She challenges him forthrightly, effectively leaving him with little choice other than to radically change his mind, something he may have acknowledged and thanked her for, but there is little chance of that being recorded in the Gospels. This must surely be one of the most empowering stories in the entire New Testament, leaving the poet wondering whether the healing of the daughter might not have been more the work of the woman herself rather than Jesus.[15]

Elisabeth Schüssler Fiorenza highlights the liberating empowerment not merely for the woman herself but also for all Gentiles — both then and now: "The Syrophenician woman whose adroit argument opened up a future of freedom and wholeness for her daughter has also become the historically still-visible advocate of such a future for Gentiles. She has become the apostolic 'foremother' of all gentile Christians."[16]

Poem 5: Another vivid story is that of the woman with the hemorrhage (Mark 5:25–34; Matt. 9:20–22; Luke 8:43–48). This woman has had a bleeding condition for twelve years (indicating a very long time). During all that time she has been castigated as ritually impure. The allusion to the money spent on doctors probably highlights the fact that many doctors would not even examine her or treat her illness because to do so would mean they would become ritually unclean themselves. Being unclean, she has been shunned and excluded for years. In all probability she has also been the subject of judgmental gossip: "What curse in her family caused her to inherit this affliction?" In the eyes of many people of her day she was a nobody (a nonperson). There must have been times when she felt incredibly lonely, forsaken, isolated, and cursed!

Then comes the miracle before the miracle! Some fierce inner intuition awakens deep within, telling her that this is her hour and that she must seize it. So through the crowd she forces her way, touching many people and *knowingly* making every one of them unclean in the process. But she does not care! Religious laws and prohibitions have to be dispensed with. This is the companionship of empowerment in all its prophetic radiance, leaving us with one of the most liberating and empowering stories in the entire New Testament.

She touches the hem of the garment of Jesus, automatically making him unclean! And as a respectable male Jew he should have castigated her for this infringement of "God's law." Instead he commends her for what she has done, subversively flying in the face of all the holy regulations. All hell is breaking loose in this story!

And he heals her! Not necessarily any strange miracle of supernatural power; perhaps, unambiguous words of subversive affirmation: "You are a beautiful God-like creature, who happens to have this human affliction in your life, but for God that is not a problem, so don't worry about it, just get on with your life." It would have been the first time she would have ever heard those words!

However we choose to understand the miracle, we need to remember that it is her miracle as much as that of Jesus. She is the one who took the unprecedented initiative. Let's never deny her that. That is the bold self-empowerment that calls forth the prophet in every God-like creature.

Poem 6: For a widow to stand up to a judge and persist in getting what she knows she is entitled to takes some courage and nerve (Luke 18:1–8). In the time of Jesus widows were sometimes revered as elders, but often dismissed as useless, since they no longer belonged to a significant male. The attitude toward them was very much one of "know your passive place and remain in it."

But not this widow! She calls the judge to accountability in terms of Torah justice. She not only denounces him but demands that he fulfill his duty — in the name of justice. Herzog captivates the scene vividly: the parable is rife with reversal and paradox. The widow is the powerful one who confronts the judge.[17] She embodies a new vision of the world, an empowering liberation for all victims of injustice and oppression.

Poems 7, 8, 9 depict the cruel objectification of women, sometimes expressed in an overspiritualizing of their existence, as in the case of Martha and Mary and the story of the widow's mite, or in the crude gossip (who's wife will she be?) recorded in Mark 12.

Poem 7: This memorable story is recorded only in Luke's Gospel (Luke 10:38; see John 12:1ff.). As noted previously, Luke does include more stories about women asserting themselves and being recognized by Jesus, but he tends to cast them in roles more restrictive than elsewhere in the New Testament. As in the other Gospels, Luke gives men names, or indicates their role, but leaves women somewhat anonymous. In his concern to show Martha and Mary's patriarchal subservience to male leadership (in this case, to Jesus), Luke ends up replacing the complementarity of mission with a dualistic juxtaposition in which both women show allegiance to Jesus, but the mutual giftedness of their missionary roles is marginalized and — at least in the case of Martha — made invisible.

In an oft-quoted article, Warren Carter seeks to take Martha out of the kitchen and allow her to become once more the disciple in active ministry described by the Greek word *diakonos,* the same word used of discipleship in Acts, indicating public ministry and not just household serving.[18] And Mary is the other half of the missionary couple, a configuration known elsewhere in the New Testament, as pointed out by Mary Rose D'Angelo: "Behind these stories is the memory of two famous women who formed a missionary partnership, like the pairs in Matt. 10:1–4. They are known and remembered as Martha the *diakonos* and Mary the sister (*adelphe*). Just as Paul signed letters as Paul the *apostolus* with a companion designated as 'the brother' (*adelphos*)."[19]

Poem 8: Note here the context in which both Mark and Luke place the story of the widow's mite (Mark 12:41–44; Luke 21:1–4): between the denunciation of the Pharisees for "taking advantage of widows and robbing them of their homes," and the denunciation of the temple (Luke 21:5ff.; Mark 13:1ff.).

Instead of this being a story for model discipleship of the obedient and faithful type, perhaps it should be understood as a subversive story with a fierce desire for justice for the poor and marginalized, represented in the person of the widow. Homilists tend to glamorize the widow in terms of her generosity and all she gave so willingly. But it is possible that she had no choice if she wanted to be in a right relationship with God as taught and promoted by the temple authorities upholding the religious convictions of the time — in which case she is being robbed of the little she had left to live on. She may well be the victim of a cruel kind of religiosity that engenders despair and guilt rather than hope and meaning.

Poem 9: All three Synoptic Gospels record the diatribe about the woman widowed seven times over (Mark 12:18–27; Matt. 22:23–33; Luke 20:27–38). Here we encounter the patriarchal preoccupation about marital privilege and the role played by the family in securing patriarchal succession. As indicated by Elisabeth Schüssler Fiorenza: "The law of levirate marriage served the purpose of continuing the patriarchal family, by securing its wealth and the inheritance within it, a concern important to the Sadducees, many of whom were upper class and priests, rich landowners living in Jerusalem."[20]

And Myers observes that the crucial issue is that of the maintenance of the socioeconomic system through the posterity of the seven sons. No concern is voiced for the barrenness of the woman, a source of ridicule and marginalization for many women of the time.[21]

Significant though these social factors are, Jesus confronts the cultural rhetoric with a prophetic challenge: if in the afterlife no one can claim possession of her as property or commodity, therefore no one ought to own or enslave her here on earth.

Poem 10: The story of the widow of Nain (Luke 7:11ff.) may have nothing to do with a miraculous raising from the dead. In all probability, the symbolic meaning takes precedence. In the time of Jesus, a widow woman who loses her only son becomes a virtual nobody. She is nobody's husband and nobody's mother, and these were the two primary roles through which her status as a woman was defined.

Consequently, not merely has she lost her husband and her only son; in fact her whole world of meaning has collapsed. She is totally bereft! Her last semblance of meaning and purpose has been snatched from her. Therefore, calling the son back to life should not be read as Jesus defying or contradicting the laws of nature, but a symbolic statement of rebirthing new life through which the woman has her dignity and status restored. Scholars note the possible parallels with Old Testament instances of women receiving back their dead, as in the case of the Shunamite woman (2 Kgs. 4:18–37), whose son was raised by Elisha.

Poems 11 and 12: In Genesis we read the story of Abraham preparing to sacrifice his son Isaac, with apparently no consultation whatever with the boy's mother. Everything is happening as if she does not exist. Concern for her feelings, her rights, her responsibilities toward the child are totally flouted.

In the New Testament we also encounter stories where the mother's role as a mother, with all the love and concern that go with it, is condemned to a kind of cruel silence, a corrosive muteness no poet or prophet can tolerate. What must it have been like to have been the mother of the man born blind (John 9:1ff.), having to endure all the taunts and gossip that ensued; and what a joy for that mother when he claims his adult self and asserts his right to speak — and his right to be!

And the mother in the story of the prodigal (Luke 15:11ff.): she is the one who would have really grieved his loss and would certainly have gone in search for him. But, alas, she is not even mentioned in the story. Let justice have its day, and let's hear her voice. It does not take too much imagination to get inside her soul.

Poem 13: Although Luke names the two disciples sent to prepare the Passover as Peter and John (Luke 22:7–13), there is little evidence in the New Testament of men preparing food for meals. There may be confusion here with the fact that two males were normally assigned the task of slaughtering the paschal lamb. Along with Robert Van Voorst I accept the suggestion that these two disciples were women, who nearly always prepared food and meals in the time of Jesus.[22]

And the issue of the man with an alabaster jar is also puzzling. Was it not always women who carried such jars? Is there a shift here to symbolic meaning suggesting that stereotypical roles are shifting under the new freedom of the companionship of empowerment?

Poem 14: Women were the first witness to the Resurrection, and if we could retrieve the true history of the time we would probably see that it was the women who kept alive the post-Calvary memory of Jesus, and in doing so, would have endured tremendous pain and social isolation. It was those same women, with a deeply integrated faith, that knew him to be alive in some radically new, inexplicable way, a countercultural view they held on to tenaciously and in time brought others around, including the disillusioned male followers, to embrace new hope for the future.

Central to that endeavor was Mary Magdalene (see John 20:11–18), the one who seems to have held the group together with a quality of steadfastness that defies all rationality. It has taken some two thousand years to acknowledge her true status as "the apostle to the apostles," a quality of apostleship, however, primarily invested in women and not in men.

1. Mary, Woman of the Body!

As a woman of the womb, I embrace what's yet to come,
And glorify the holy source a-singing.
My past I can't deny as my genes do verify,
I'm a woman, wife and mother to the living.

And my skin is very dark as my origins do mark.
Yes, I am the Black Madonna from the start.
Neither European nor white, nor colonial in spite,
Standing solidly with people of true heart.

The blessings of the flesh as a woman young and fresh,
I have borne human offspring in my stride.
No immaculate conceived, all that nonsense so deceived,
I hold maternal instinct with great pride.

My Son they say was special, as declared in holy writ
And he turned out much different than I'd hoped.
His inner restless searching led him on the road to preaching
And I scarcely understood a word he said.

Not much into religion, he denounced the laws as legion.
He caused many disagreements in our home.

I could not get him married, though women round him tarried.
Mid my offspring the strangest one by far.

I wish he stopped the preaching and especially the teaching,
So embarrassing within the neighborhood.
But I never anticipated a death so desecrated,
Crucified upon a morbid piece of wood.

They say he had a message that would change society's image
And some women started quickly on the new.
I said I would support them, though I could not understand them,
Talking visions of a kingdom to renew.

Bemused along the journey, I watched the men returning.
That leading guy called Peter seemed so strange.
He found it hard to function, with women in conjunction,
And the Kingdom vision quickly he deranged.

And I hate the power and glory in that Queen of Heaven story,
Declaring I assumed above the sky.
I'm a proudly earthly woman, more at home in cosmic union,
Please allow me to be human as I try.

And forget that white-faced Mary, veiled and scaled to look contrary,
Emulating colonizer's deep desire.
I'm a dark-skinned bodied woman, with erotic zeal to summon
As a mother to the planet's future fire.

2. On Being a Whole Woman!

Surrounded by townsfolk, with Jesus astride,
The voice of a woman echoed home from the wild.
Declaring a blessing on the womb of his birth,
And the breasts that he sucked when he first came on earth.
What a prospect to have been that woman!

In that time a woman, her task was clear-cut,
To prop up the race by the sons she begot.
Her womb and her breasts were parts for a task

But the truth of her wholeness it often got lost.
What a burden to have been a woman!

And Jesus retorted with insight and grace
Inviting her wholeness — in its rightful place.
Not just womb and breasts make woman complete
But embodied presence with wisdom replete.
What a challenge to have been a woman!

And the good news of hope is not just for the men.
Often heard by the women with deeper intent,
And proclaimed in the birthing of all that is new,
Beyond womb and breasts is a far deeper view.
What a privilege to have been a woman!

The birthing of hope in the Gospel of life
Is a call to us all to grow and to thrive.
With the fullness of woman and the fullness of man
Co-creating a future with grace to expand.
A blessing for both man and woman!

3. Simon, Can You See?

Can you see this person standing here, a woman of full truth
With the elegance of womanhood, richly feminine imbued?
With the beauty of her passion, erotic to the core
And the birthing-power within her inviting to explore!
Simon, can you see? Can you see? Can you see?

Can you see the tears of centuries of patriarchal woe
And the courage it must take her for integrity of soul?
Can you see the waves of flowing hair with which she wiped my feet
And the kisses of her intimacy, making healing so replete?
Simon, can you see?...

Can you see her hospitality, her warmth, her embrace;
Her ability for birthing as a mother to each race?
A living icon of the ages, the Goddess we long have known,

Maligned and desecrated by the dogmas YOU have sown!
Simon, can you see?…

Can you see her jar of ointment, anointing to empower
Those excluded by oppression, overwhelmed and weighed down?
Can you see her gracious pouring out, abundant as of yore
While you stand there in judgment, a pontificating bore!
Simon, can you see?…

Her eyes though filled with weeping tears are contemplating clear.
She can see right through the lot of us, our judgments and our fear.
Remember Holy Wisdom—she embodies it anew
And she radiates sheer goodness for creation to imbue!
Simon, can you see?…

She has known the ups and downs of life, the sinful and the free.
And forgiven much, she's loving much—for empowering liberty.
The system can't contain her and the freedom she proclaims,
She's a living revelation where love and justice reigns.
Simon, can you see?…

Long after we have run our course and echoes fade in time
Her name will be invoked afresh in Scripture and in rhyme.
And the alabaster jar she holds will replenish many souls,
And where the Gospel is proclaimed, her fame will be disclosed.
And, then, Simon, you might see; I hope you will see!

4. A Woman's Dogged Faith

They call her the woman from Syrophoenicia,
Her daughter demented with anguish and pain.
Persistently anxious, pursuing every option,
Low though her status and labeled a Gentile.
But deep in her heart a breakthrough she can see.

For Jesus the struggle is also precarious,
Haunted by Israel's desire to be first.
They duly reserve him for the lost house of Israel,

Dismissing all others his people to please.
But deep in her heart a breakthrough she can see.

"I know your dilemma with the people of Israel.
I know they oft feel we infringe their domain.
Like dogs 'neath the table, the children's food taking,
They resent our presence 'cause we're not the true race.
But deep in my heart a breakthrough I can see."

"Forgive me, dear woman, lest you feel I exclude you;
your dogged persistence I deeply admire.
The crumbs from the table sustain you in wisdom,
You drink from the wells of endurance and hope.
And deep in your heart a breakthrough you can see."

"Go home to your daughter and embrace her with wisdom;
Sustain her with crumbs that will heal and restore.
Your faith can move mountains, O Miracle Woman,
YOU do the healing and I will support.
For deep in your heart a breakthrough you can see."

"Now I and my daughter are gathered at table.
We're nourished with crumbs that feed and sustain.
In union with women, oppressed and excluded,
Desiring a home where all can be one.
For deep in our hearts a breakthrough we can see."

5. The Woman with the Hemorrhage

'Twas awkward and painful, but worse still 'twas shameful,
This curse I was carrying for so many years.
The clergy denounced me and the doctors renounced me,
While young guys pronounced me a dirty old slag.
I never even realized a power from within.

To the wind I threw caution, fed up with depression
And broke all the rules by joining the crowd.
There were stories of healing which got my head reeling

Through the crowd I was feeling my way to the source.
Determined to awaken my power from within.

My wisdom assured me that a mere touch had cured me.
I clung to his garment as hard as I could.
His gaze it surprised me as wholeness now seized me,
I stood mesmerized that 'twould happen to me.
Enamored and blessed by a power from within.

His words were not many, but his eyes were uncanny
Right into my heart came the gaze of true peace.
What a load he had lifted, what hope he had shifted,
And the healing he gifted I'll never forget.
So much was achieved through the power from within.

The healer that's wounded can now remain grounded
And undo oppression against mighty odds.
And you that are wounded must never be hounded
By people confounded inflicting your pain.
Like me, you can call forth the power from within.

6. The Widow Who Kept Up the Pressure

I know I am only a widow
Some think they can quickly dismiss.
But I've heard of a New Reign of freedom
Empowered with the grace to persist.
I will not take "No" for an answer,
From emperor, ruler, or priest.
So, this arrogant judge better wake up,
Or a great deal of time he will waste.

Once a victim of male domination,
In a culture addicted to power.
For years I have lived in the shadows,
But I know this is liberty's hour.
All I ask for is rendering justice,
Please, treat me with full dignity.

I'm a full being of God as a woman
And I want every creature set free.

He tried me to fob off so often,
But in time became tired of the game.
And though grudgingly then condescended
I cherish the power I regained.
For some it takes years of hard struggle
To break through a system so raw.
To mobilize more our resources
Is the challenge upon which to draw.

I never had dreamed it would happen
The Gospels my story reclaim.
Although only Luke does record it
And as usual doesn't mention my name.
We, women, must keep on persisting
This freedom that Jesus has sought,
Must still be more widely implanted,
In action, in word, and in thought.

7. Martha and Mary

These are women of wisdom and grace!
Companions in mission diverse roles to lead.
The false opposition we quickly impose,
While their mutual empowerment we tend to misread.
One renders a service to welcome the guest,
pouring her heart out in kind.
No wonder she resents the sibling that opts
just to sit there and wisdom imbibe.

The part that was chosen by Mary the quiet
can easily be misconstrued.
Between the two sisters there is no divide.
both are gifted and richly imbued.
If this was the journey that led to the cross,

and Jesus had glimpsed it his fate,
Then Mary had chosen the wholesome response,
attending a friend to death's gate.

His heart would be heavy and weary in soul,
and the thought of indulging in food,
was the last thing on earth he could now entertain,
but to Martha he would not be rude.
A poignant vibration runs right through this tale,
of affection so tender and true.
The heart of the Gospel that echoes through time,
neither Martha nor Mary will rue.

And where in our time amid carnage so cruel
do we hallow the women so brave,
who bind up the wounds and render true love
our world in turmoil to save!

8. Robbing Even a Widow's Mite!

She's oft admired by homilists for giving all she had.
And allegedly she gave it all, her mite to mighty God.
And we're told the temple treasury was the focus of her giving,
And it sounds like they don't give a damn what she has left for living.
Having stripped her of all she had to placate some wicked God.

We need to give discerning care to the context of the tale,
How widows oft are victimized and robbed of all their bail.
So cruel the mercy she must gain to win her way into God's reign.
No wonder Jesus pounces and the temple fierce denounces,
For robbing her of all she had to placate some wicked God.

Suspicion's hermeneutic we need at times employ,
'Cause holy writ's corruption can be devious and sly.
And care to take collude we not, with crippling guilt and fear,
That have no place in God's New Reign, new life and hope declare.
And retrieve the widow's dignity from the temple's wicked God.

9. To Whom Does She Belong?

It's the story of a woman and her seven husbands all,
And the death of their fertility is the curse on her befall.
While Resurrection rhetoric so deviously invoked
Casts patriarchal shadows ensuring truth is choked.
And amazingly the system continues to oppress.

The rhetoric's seductive around the woman's plight,
It's loaded with oppression, misogyny so trite.
As long as there are male heirs to propagate the race,
Her significance is minimal, an object of disgrace.
And amazingly the system continues to oppress.

Their interest in the woman betrays a morbid flaw,
Her death subdued in gossip — on which they only draw.
Till Jesus trumps reversal and calls their faith to task,
Their convoluted arguments forever are unmasked.
And amazingly the system continues to oppress.

The living God adorns life in this time and beyond,
The risen hope already here for those who comprehend.
This woman too is destined as angels are set free,
And misogyny outwitted in the power of God's decree.
And amazingly the system continues to oppress.

Some day when we awaken to the Reign of God on earth,
And every being is cherished in the wisdom of the heart.
And tribalistic rhetoric no longer can endure,
As Gospel love and justice are nourished to the fore.
Then, amazingly, the system no longer can oppress.

10. Bereft at the Gate of Nain

Imagine the plight of a woman bereft,
Already a sorrowful widow.
And now with the death of her one only son,
The dark clouds are casting their shadow.

Unless she belonged to man as a wife,
Or can claim to be somebody's mother.
She's really a nobody—completely bereft,
Her value and worth they will smother.

The Gospel of Luke is at pains to reclaim
The status of women subdued.
And this is a story rebirthing anew
A cursed isolation removed.

The story has echoes of others revived
In what seems like defying laws of nature.
But this is an action of prophetic hope
And rebirthing is the central feature.

Rebirthing takes place when Jesus presents
A son that's raised up to his mother.
They both are rebirthed and raised to new life,
A freedom that's destined forever!

11. Reflections from the Mother of the Blind Man

What a grueling we all got that day!
The family curse that haunted my years,
The guilt and the shame and the petrifying fears.
In fact, he was not blind from birth,
But nobody trusted my word.
In the shadows we stood, condemned from the start,
Mid the blindness of cruel desperation!

What a grueling we all got that day!
"It must be his parents who passed on the curse,
They must take the blame for a plight that is worse."
My husband was numb to the core,
And my anger was growing by the score.
To label the curse in which he's blindly caught,
A scapegoat of cruel desperation.

What a grueling we all got that day!
His friendship with Jesus was also disgraced,
While the ritual with clay was mocked and defaced.
But I saw a new look in his eyes;
It pierced through their darkness inside.
And the lid of oppression was loosened at last,
In a shatter beyond desperation.

What a grueling we all got that day!
Till the adult inside began to explode
He'll speak for himself as an adult so bold.
But the adult they can't entertain,
Too much for the power games they feign.
And my boy that was blind so proudly acclaims:
"You, too, want to be his disciples?"

What a grueling he gave them that day!
My son who had suffered for so many years,
The guilt and the shame and the petrifying fears!
The confident adult comes forth,
Co-dependency yields to new growth.
For the New Reign of God turns right upside down,
The culture of cruel desperation.

12. The Prodigal Mother Has Her Say

At first I tried to tell myself it was not what he meant.
And in calmer times of reason he surely would repent.
In common with his father was this explosive streak,
Perhaps for just a few hours or at very most a week.
Something told me it was different this time round.

Not seen him for ten days and didn't hear a word.
Even my boisterous husband sensed my panic and my dread.
What if he's run out of money or of food!
What if he's attacked, by vagabonds pursued!
The worry of it all gave me many sleepless nights.

Alas, the months went by, my grieving heart was sore.
Our neighbors and our leaders had searched each lengthy shore.
I know I had to do it despite all who disagreed,
I headed for the road myself with very little lead.
A brokenhearted mother defying the odds of hope.

Those city streets were frightening, where homeless people roam.
Their stories all so poignant on why they too left home.
I showed them Nathan's picture and thankfully a few
Had seen him round the market, helping the fishing crew.
My darling wayward son — was still alive!

I talked to many fisherfolk to get some vital clue.
It took some weeks of searching and eventually got through.
We cried our hearts together, so painful an embrace.
Two wearied souls now rescued by mercy of God's grace.
And we faced for home together with hearts of such relief.

The rest is in Luke's Gospel and the welcome he received.
A repentant mellowed father, so reckless mid his grief.
And the other son in turmoil who could not comprehend
Once again I was the go-between his anger to attend.
Does a mother ever get a break from caring for her flock?

The story's reputation of a father and his son,
I wonder why the writer says so little 'bout their mum.
I'm not into adulation, but I do appreciate
A little recognition and the difference I do make.
Perhaps some day the Gospels will acknowledge us as well.

13. Preparing for the Passover

Who are these two disciples, the Passover meal prepare?
And who's the one along the street with an alabaster jar?
It sounds like role reversal is blowing the plot apart
And the open common table is winning through at last.
The patriarchal slaughtered lamb has no more blood to shed!
And the feast of liberation will leave many folks in dread.

The food of preparation throughout the Gospel lore
Is distinctively prerogative, unique to woman's role.
So the people sent with dignity this final meal prepare
Must surely be the women—to name them we must dare!
The patriarchal slaughtered lamb has no more blood to shed.
But the baker-woman's table will nourish us with bread.

The night before Passover time anticipates a feast,
While the women sieve the harvest flour and add the rising yeast.
With fruits and herbs and wine to drink, the table now prepared,
In the blessings of abundant life discipleship is shared.
The patriarchal slaughtered lamb has no more blood to shed.
This is the new Jerusalem—Resurrection lies ahead!

And the women who prepared the feast
With birthpangs of the rising yeast
Must carry forth what food sustains,
For slaughtered lambs leave scant remains.
They'll meet again as male disciples sink in doubt,
Proclaiming to the world that Risen hope has broken out!

14. First Witness to the Resurrection

Perplexed in the garden where death and life entwine,
Embalming all the paradox of Mary's tearful gaze.
She stands before an open tomb,
While behind a gardener in full bloom,
Begins to weave a pattern, an empowering Easter maze.

Angelic voices rumbled within her grieving heart,
Distorting and disturbing the comfort of her grief.
Her bleary gaze moves right around,
She stares aghast on holy ground.
While the one who calls her "woman" will resurrect relief.

With a startling glimpse of insight, the scales fall from her eyes,
Like a mystic probe in consciousness gone wild.
She's at home in true fulfillment,

An abyss of real contentment,
But within transfigured ecstasy she cannot long abide.

She's conferred in her apostleship and sent forth to the rest.
We waste no time in resurrected hope.
And tears of loss and ecstasy,
Will serve the call to prophesy,
Inviting all the nations, the Good News to invoke.

The landscape of her mission lies betwixt the dark and light,
With empowerment that's already broken through.
Some disciples will reject her,
At the margins they'll accept her,
And religion will need centuries her vision to imbue.

Chapter Thirteen

The (Dis)Empowerment of the Cross

Poetry heals the wounds inflicted by reason.
— NOVALIS

Unless we speak poetically, we invite terrible reductions.
— WALTER BRUEGGEMANN

For many centuries, Christians were taught and believed that it is the death and resurrection of Jesus that really matter — all the rest is a lead-up to that final sacrificial act of redemption in which Jesus somehow makes up to God for all our sins and procures our eternal salvation.

In recent decades there has been a significant move away from that perspective, rapidly being replaced by the understanding that salvation and redemption belong primarily to the LIFE of Jesus and not to his *death*.[1] The untimely death is the price paid for a life radically and prophetically lived. The power brokering system became so scared of his ministry of empowerment that they cornered him at an opportune moment, not to punish him, but exterminate him. In the words of Rosemary Radford Ruether:

> It is not Jesus' suffering and death that are redemptive, but his life as a praxis of protest against injustice and solidarity in defense of life. . . . Suffering is a factor in the liberation process, not as a means of redemption, but as the risk that one takes when one struggles to overcome unjust systems whose beneficiaries resist change. The means of redemption is conversion, opening up to one another, changing systems of distorted relations, creating loving and life-giving communities of people here and now, not getting oneself tortured to death.[2]

What is radically redemptive, liberating, and empowering in the earthly presence of Jesus is all in his *life,* not in his death, which was a despicable, brutal suppression typically meted out to slaves, bandits, and troublemakers. According to James Dunn: "Crucifixion was a Roman form of punishment for recalcitrant slaves and political rebels."[3] Malina and Rohrbaugh state: "Rigidly hierarchical societies such as those under Roman imperial rule in the ancient Mediterranean world do not allow for trials of inferiors; instead they have accusations and punishments.... Crucifixion was considered the appropriate punishment for slaves."[4]

Resurrection, in turn, is not so much about the vindication of the crucified one; rather it is an archetypal affirmation of a life fully and radically lived. As Christians, therefore, our primary commitment must be to the radical empowerment that leads to the fullness of life, with a view to eliminating all unjust suffering and meaningless death in our world. The image of the crucified Christ may indeed bring comfort and consolation to the sufferer, but it will never procure liberation from suffering which is a primary goal of the companionship of empowerment.

◆ ◆ ◆

The poems of this section are distinctly different from most of the poetry (and art) that exalts and acclaims the greatness of the crucified one, often focusing on the gory details of human brutality as in Mel Gibson's *The Passion of the Christ*. The poems strive to reclaim suffering as an integral dimension of liberation and empowerment, and not as an end in itself.

Poem 1 describes Jesus being anointed in preparation for what lies ahead (Mark 14:3–9; Matt. 26:6–13; Luke 7:36–38; John 12:1–8). If such an anointing took place, and there would be some cultural precedent for it, then almost certainly Mary Magdalene is the person who would have conferred it. When material is recorded in the Gospels for which we cannot find factual historical evidence, we have both a spiritual and intellectual responsibility to find alternative explanations. At this juncture, the archetypal meaning, which tends to be suppressed, is perhaps the one that should first be honored, and particularly when dealing with an event that carries deep mystical meaning.

Poem 2: The short passage from the Letter to the Philippians (2:5–11) on the self-emptying of Jesus (the kenotic theory) has had more exegetical commentary than almost any other New Testament text. Sarah Coakley provides a comprehensive overview of the various theories, condensing them into four main approaches:

1. emptying out of preexistent divine power to facilitate the act of redemption;

2. pretending to relinquish divine power while actually retaining it (as Gnostic redeemer);

3. affirming that God and Jesus have nothing to do with power as understood by mortals;

4. revealing divine power to be intrinsically humble rather than grasping.

Coakley herself opts for a fifth interpretation: rather than deny or condemn human vulnerability, Jesus fully embraces it and uses it as a means for empowerment through a new solidarity with all human suffering.[5]

Poem 3: The scene here is that of the agony in the garden of Gethsemane (Mark 14:32–42; Matt. 26:36–46; Luke 22:40–46), one of those moments in which we see the human face of God enduring all the terror, fear, and anguish so well known to us in those painful moments of absolute abandonment. Incarnation embraces everything that constitutes the human condition, including the experience of absolute darkness and utter despair.

Poem 4: Jesus was condemned to death as a common criminal and as such would have had no trials. The Gospel writers provide trials, still clinging to the notion that Jesus really was a king, and as such would have had trials. What is on trial is the violent power of patriarchy itself,[6] and the six recorded trials provide a vivid portrayal of its crazy recklessness:

1. First Religious Trial (Jewish): Annas (John 18:12–14). *Decision:* No signal given to execute Jesus.

2. Second Religious Trial: Caiaphas (Matt. 26:57–68). *Decision:* Death sentence on the charge of blasphemy, because Jesus proclaimed himself the Messiah, God the Son.

3. Third Religious Trial: Sanhedrin (Matt. 27:1–2; Luke 22:63–71). *Decision:* Death sentence legalized.

4. First Civil Trial (Roman): Pilate (John 18:28–38). *Decision:* Not guilty.

5. Second Civil Trial: Herod (Luke 23:6–12). *Decision:* Not guilty.

6. Third Civil Trial: Pilate again (John 18:39–19:6). *Decision:* Not guilty, but turned over to be crucified (Matt. 27:26).[7]

We also need to remember that common criminals usually were not buried. Frequently, they were left on the cross to rot, or their crucified bodies were dumped in an open pit and devoured by wild beasts or birds. Gruesome though it sounds, we have to face the fact that this too is probably what would have happened to Jesus, unless his followers somehow succeeded in retrieving his body (against heavy odds). As suggested in the next section, the women (standing at a distance) are possible candidates for that incredible achievement.

Poem 5: Crucifixion was a brutal, horrible death without dignity or meaning. Malina and Rohrbaugh claim that "executions served as a crude form of public entertainment.... Death by crucifixion was often slow and protracted. The power-less victims suffered bodily distortions, loss of bodily control, and enlargement of the penis.... In many cases, victims were denied honorable burial; corpses were left on display and devoured by carrion birds and scavenger animals."[8]

Exalting the death of Jesus, whether for spiritual or theological reasons, pos-sibly gained significance because of the cruel pain and persecution Christians often endured in early Christian times. Brock and Parker provide a detailed review of Christian art in the first Christian millennium, indicating that the focus on the death of Jesus is a post-atonement phenomenon, with little religious significance before the tenth century.[9] Today, as Grace Jantzen suggests, we need to shift the emphasis from mortality to natality (that is, flourishing): birthing the companion-ship of empowerment in order to enhance the flourishing of all life is our primary goal as a Christian people.[10] Death then can be seen for what it really is: an inte-gral dimension of the cycle of birth-death-rebirth, and not some proverbial curse caused by the sins of humanity.

Poem 6: Did Jesus forgive Judas? If Jesus came back today would he still for-give Judas? To both questions the answer is an unambiguous *yes!* Otherwise, the challenge to love one's enemies loses all real meaning. Judas seems to have en-visioned Jesus as the one who eventually would perform a mighty act of rescue that would once and forever destroy the forces of evil and initiate a dramatic reign of God in the world. In all probability, this too was the messianic dream all the apostles shared. Judas just took it so much more literally, even to the point of self-ruination.

It looks like Judas might have figured out that since Jesus was not working the great rescue in his lifetime, it was going to happen at the hour of death about which he does seem to have spoken to the disciples. So Judas reckons: if that is going to be the great moment of liberation, why not try and bring it closer? Why not use the money to set up a seditious plot whereby Jesus would be captured sooner and then, faced with the prospect of untimely execution, he would work the great miracle to disempower all his enemies.

In this scenario, Judas would have meant well, and if we had been with him at the time we might well have agreed with him. But a larger logic was at play, which neither Judas nor any of the other disciples (male) seem to have grasped. And when Judas realized the awful mistake he had made, understandably he was plunged into a despair too deep for words, in the face of which he committed suicide.

Would Jesus forgive Judas? Has Jesus forgiven Judas? If Judas can't be forgiven, then "love your enemies" is just empty rhetoric, and God's unconditional love is nothing more than an empty platitude.

1. Mary's Eschatological Anointing

Leave her alone, she knows what she's about!
My head with oil she does anoint,
She knows the game is up — time to appoint.
This darkest hour she can withstand.
And waver now I must not,
'neath the empowering touch,
of her firm, gentle hand.

Leave her alone, no money wasted in this precious time.
Embalming odor to fulfill,
A house so full, a death so chill.
She knows the wisdom to anticipate
And waver now I must not
Empowered I must go forth,
They're waiting at the gate.

Leave her alone and spare her all the empty rhetoric,
She knows the score, this time of destiny,
And she'll survive the cruelest felony.
As others flee, too scared to hang around.
And waver now I must not
'cause by the cross she stands,
Anointing holy ground.

Leave her alone till Resurrection's dawn
And watch the garden of her painful stroll,
The breaking waters of her birthing role.

Apostolic succession is hers to wield.
And waver now I must not
With wisdom so replete,
A faithful future is guaranteed.

2. Emptying in Vulnerability

Long have the scholars debated the text
On whether or not I relinquished
The power that uniquely would make me divine,
Poured out but never extinguished.

And what was poured out is the other concern,
My nature as human-divine?
Or was it a case of renouncing the power
That patriarchs give the male line?

While scholars can look at a text in detail,
The story behind it can differ.
And the obvious wisdom is easily lost
Analyzing the details forever.

The text is an icon of ultimate truth,
Uniting human and divine.
A God who is vulnerable right to the core,   .
The face of compassion sublime.

The suffering pain that everyone knows
Is also God's suffering heart.
There is no distinction in the spectrum of life,
The human-and-God counterpart.

The liturgy song from Philippians Two,
Rewards with exalting on high.
But that is the blessing that everyone shares
As we grow in the pain of dark night.

And the healer that's wounded is called to repair
The suffering and pain of our world.

Diminish the havoc that oppression reaps,
Bringing justice that endures forever.

And never adopt the holiness code,
To suffer just for its own sake.
I came to get rid of all meaningless pain
A mission in which you too partake.

A heart that is vulnerable, broken yet whole,
A mission with hope to imbue.
It's God's heart and your heart united as one,
God's dream for the earth ever new.

3. The Loneliness of Abandonment

'Twas a killer in that garden; I was nearly sweating blood,
And I cursed the very one who brought me here.
And the three I had relied on to sustain in my ordeal
Were a massive disappointment in the end.

I wondered if the whole thing, a failure out and out,
Another sage deluded in the end.
And the massive crowds that followed, did they really comprehend?
I never thought I'd pay a price like this.

Instead of those three idiots in dreamland so intent
I should have asked the women for support.
But now I guess the die is cast, and here I am alone.
Not even heaven's rumbling to assure.

I don't want to go through it all, but it looks as if I must,
I wish this cup of suffering could pass.
While the spirit is so willing, the flesh is weak indeed,
I feel betrayed by everyone at hand.

What oft I preached to others, I had better self-apply
And take the leap of faith I oft proclaimed.
So welcome be your holy will, I place my hands in yours.
But for God's sake, hurry up, and bring me through!

4. Jesus on Trial

My name is Annas,
Five years of priestly height beneath my belt,
Safeguarding the light of truth even in the dark of night.
Messianic suitors seek to undermine
What we must safely guard,
And mock the very ground upon which these impostors stand.
The cheeky bastard refused to answer,
No respect for priesthood or old age.
But the High Priest has power to wield,
And will not yield to this daring, staring insolence.

My name is Caiaphas,
Chosen to serve the God of rendering account.
The inner sanctum of my temple space
This pervert Jesus has transgressed with such disgrace.
One man must die and him it is by due decree.
A threat to God, he blasphemes against our holy nation,
With no respect at all for godly regulation.
Convoke the Council of those who wisely judge,
This curse upon our people the time has come to purge.

We are the Council of the High Priest,
Our eyes are blearied from the sleep we've missed.
Refusing all our questions, so stubbornly resist,
So arrogant and ignorant before our godly power,
So reckless this disruption throughout the nightly hour.
The high priest has pronounced, so now proceed,
And send him on to Pilate as holy laws decree.

My name is Pilate,
Honored by the holy seal of Roman Right.
I too have lost much sleep on this frenetic night.
But messengers from Rome seek daily checks
To see how well I handle these messianic quirks.
I audit all his movements and his flair,
And I wish I had his wisdom and ability to care.
But empowering all that rabble for me is quite a scare.

So I must save my skin — and him as well,
If I can manage it! Perhaps have Herod quell
This freak from Galilee wherein he's known so well.

My name is Herod,
Blessed with God's kingly might to rule,
And so glad indeed to see this messianic fool.
The benefit of doubt, I'll justly try to meet,
Perhaps, he'll work a miracle, a very special treat!
But standing there in silence I will not tolerate.
This guy made allegations and them we must get straight.
'Cause this time round 'tis reckoning — I know it all too well!
Let Pilate do the dirty work — condemn this twit to hell!

My name is Pilate,
I wish I was as clever as that vixen of a king,
And my wife is in a panic saying I must not do a thing.
And they won't accept Barabbas, the scapegoat of relief,
So what the hell am I to do — this quandary I've conceived?
I know the guy is innocent, but I must save my back
And pacify the powers in Rome, the odds against me stack.
I hate being in a corner — when there's nothing else to do,
So TAKE HIM YOURSELVES AND CRUCIFY HIM, you f---ing shameless crew!

(Some years later)

They haunt me still those piercing eyes astride a piece of wood,
And what followed feels like rubbing salt into a gaping wound.
As I watch those women leading, with Magdalene to the fore.
How the hell did SHE get it right, allegedly a whore!
And Peter with his fishing gang in time they joined the band.
Not even my mighty empire could halt them in command.
So, Caesar and Augustus and yours truly shedding tears
Must watch this mighty empire crumbling mid our fears.
It pains me to admit it, but I cannot keep it in:
I knew that guy was special — and of course did Magdalene!

5. *Saved by My Death on a Cross?*

There's a lurid fascination with what happened in the end,
The deadly plight for thousands at the time.
And continues till the present in the pain and agony,
Of the many who are tortured and maligned.

> CHORUS:
> *So, can you keep on claiming that my cross was victory,*
> *Or propose redemptive value for this pain?*
> *And the butchery you've justified by virtue of the cross,*
> *A sordid mess, so tragic and in vain.*

Like many other criminals denouncing kingly rule,
I met my doom a gibbet on the hill.
Deprived of all the trappings the Gospels 'lucidate,
My death was quick and brutal in the end. CHORUS.

The early Christian people, persecution as their lot,
The cult of being a martyr was the prize.
A desperate search for meaning in a culture of such pain,
Glorified my crucifixion to the heights. CHORUS.

The gift of God's salvation, redemption all replete,
It radiates the fullness of my life.
The vision of the Kingdom as clear as I could state,
Would liberate from every kind of strife. CHORUS.

The suffering that matters is the context of my life,
As the seeds of love and justice start to flower.
My death is just a consequence of daring to empower
Cut short by panic brokers scared for power. CHORUS.

And the Resurrection breakthrough which you link in with my death
Belongs instead to life that's full abloom.
God's ultimate endorsement of everything I did
In a lifetime dedicated to the new! CHORUS.

6. To Judas, with Love!

It seems you were the black sheep for predilection's store,
The one who always got it wrong in holy writ and lore,
A victim and a scapegoat from the start.

You were good at handling money, although greedy on the way.
Your heart was very human, so easily did stray.
But forgiveness has a place for you as well.

I have always given ones like you the benefit of doubt,
Though the writers of the Gospels, they fail to point this out.
So, Judas, here's the verdict of appeal.

Literalism and love of money seem to be your fall from grace,
Misreading all the evidence according to your pace.
The plan of God was different from what you so ill-conceived.

You planned to hand me over in dramatic revelry,
Assuming I would work the plot of divine delivery,
Be the hero you mistakenly set up.

And when your hopes were dashed in vain, and you felt all betrayed,
Your pride was crushed and shattered, your truth was badly frayed,
Your darkest hour of absolute despair.

The others, too, had fled that night; they could not stay the pace.
You were not the only traitor in that dislocating space.
At least you had some reasons to justify your deeds.

So raise your heart my broken friend, don't hang your head in shame,
And forgive as you're forgiven — we can start afresh again.
For no one is excluded from the clasp of healing grace.

Chapter Fourteen

Resurrection as Cosmic Empowerment

Poetry at its best calls forth our deep being, bids us to live by its promptings; it dares us to break free from the safe strategies of the cautious mind; it calls to us, like the wild geese, from an open sky. —ROGER HOUSDEN

Increasingly, Christians are reluctant to equate Resurrection with the resuscitation of a dead body. Instead many opt for the view that it is more about a profound conversion of heart on the part of the disciples whereby they believed Jesus to be radically alive, even more so than during his earthly embodiment. After a detailed review of scholarly opinion, James G. D. Dunn concludes that the Resurrection is about something that happened to Jesus rather than to the disciples.[1] Yet, as a final word he states: "The resurrection of Jesus is not so much a criterion of faith as a paradigm for hope" (879).

Although I favor the view of Resurrection being about the followers, rather than about Jesus himself, such is the profound nature of this archetypal experience, I hesitate to speculate about its nature, either then or now. The Christian tradition tends to link the Resurrection with the *death* of Jesus; surely, it should be linked more explicitly with the *life* of Jesus — the jewel in the crown of a life radically and richly lived. The Gospel accounts themselves, especially the appearance stories, are loaded with the awakening of the new, the will-to-life that poetry of every age proclaims and celebrates.

◆ ◆ ◆

The poems in this section are merely an attempt to give voice to those left largely voiceless in the Gospel accounts, primarily the women, and notably Mary Magdalene.[2] Were it not for the critical role played by those women, despite a number of complex issues related to such a role,[3] it is indeed possible that Resurrection itself, and the church that arises thereafter, might never have come into being. Perhaps it's the women, and not the men, to whom we owe apostolic succession!

Poem 1: If Jesus was killed as a common criminal (and particularly at a politically tense time like that of Passover), he, too, would have suffered the plight of other criminals: his body would have been either hurriedly buried by the authorities or, more likely, dumped in a common pit for wild animals to devour. If he did get a proper burial, as the Gospels indicate, the chances are that it was the women, "watching from afar" (Mark 15:40) and working against heavy odds, who somehow succeeded in retrieving his body for burial.[4] When all others had fled, the women held on, and from the depths of that incredible pain and darkness hold their nerve till the gray light of another paradigm pierces their darkness — and the rest is Christian history!

Poem 2: In the closing decades of the twentieth century, embracing the provocative insight of Elisabeth Schüssler Fiorenza,[5] many scholars began to adopt Mary Magdalene as *the apostle to the apostles* and proceeded to mount a formidable array of literature to substantiate that claim.[6] Although hard historical fact is difficult to come by, growing evidence that a deliberate subversion of the female disciples took place, combined with the intuitive wisdom of the researchers themselves, makes this relatively new theory compelling, exciting, and empowering.

Already in the *Gospel of Thomas,* and in other apocryphal Gospels, we find allusions to the growing tensions between Mary and Peter.[7] What would that have been like after the death of Jesus? And what might their first encounter in the resurrected space have felt like? The imagination of the poet is necessary to plumb these depths.

Poem 3: This is one of the first poems I ever wrote, in December 1987, as news broke of the first remarkable heart-and-lung transplant operation in the Harefield Hospital in London. The beneficiary was a young Scottish girl, Samantha Dawkins, in what is known as a "domino transplant": they removed her healthy heart and infected lungs and replaced them with healthy heart-and-lung organs. The groundbreaking surgery was performed by the world-renowned Professor Magdi Yacoub.

Unfortunately, Samantha survived for only two years, having contracted a serious virus in 1989. Meanwhile her healthy heart had been donated to Andrew Wilson, now thirty years of age and living in the UK. While together at the Harefield, Samantha and Andrew formed a very close friendship and appeared together on TV shows. A remarkable story, graced with the paradox of death and resurrection.

Poem 4: The story of the Emmaus journey (Luke 24:13–35) begins with two people, one named and the other not, suggesting that it might have been a husband and wife. So, let's imagine what Mrs. Cleopas was like. Must we not presume that she was one of the female disciples engaging the archetypal breakthrough with insight, courage, and vision? And in that process she is probably dragging her husband along—into the faith that will also set him free!

Poem 5: The story of Jesus walking on the water (Mark 6:47–52; Matt. 14:22–27; John 6:16–21) has long puzzled scholars. Patrick J. Madden claims that what is being described in this story was first and foremost a post-Resurrection event (or experience) that found its way into the story of the earthly life of Jesus.[8] John Dominic Crossan[9] supports this view as does the Catholic scholar John P. Meier, who writes: "The walking on the water is more likely from start to finish a creation of the early Church, a Christological confession in narrative form."[10]

Like several of the other post-Resurrection appearances, we are dealing with an archetypal story carrying deep reassurance and the capacity to empower. The power is within the story itself and is best accessed by prioritizing a mythic (poetic) interpretation rather than opting for literal meaning.

1. Women Watching Far and Near!

Standing some way off, mid bleary eyes and darkness,
Impeded by the military whose task they can't obstruct.
And when death is duly registered, from the cross a body swiped
For the waiting howling animals round a common pit they gripe.
But the women mid the darkness fierce,
Engaging eyes of armor pierce,
They defy the powers so sturdy, as they bargain for his body.
Every fiber of their beings they risk,
To see justice done once more.

In the dark and cold of Calvary, they move closer by the inch
To retrieve a broken body from nihilistic doom.
Round a brokenhearted mother who never understood
The crazy life her son took on, defying his Jewish brood.
She held him close in stared relief,
At least he's saved from mauling teeth.
By defying the powers so sturdy, they have now reclaimed his body,
And proceed to bury hurriedly
Their shattered broken dream.

There is yet one consolation, a glimmer of small hope,
As they prepare the spices, their duty to fulfill.
In shattered fear and grieving, a tomb unmarked they see,
Where they thought the body buried, laid to rest by due decree.
But an open, empty chasm ripped dashing hopes apart,
And the sorrow of the moment could hardly be more stark.
They defy the powers so sturdy, and in absence of a body,
Face the frightening outer darkness
On the verge of sheer despair.

Resurrection space is frightening when light unmasks the dawn,
For the once familiar world is shattered to the core.
There's no point now in holding on to all they thought was real,
Consumed by fertile emptiness they sprout another seed.
So the women pause to embrace a new surrender,
As echoes reverberate, they do indeed remember!
They defy the powers so sturdy, rising up within the body
And the radiance of risen hope
Begins to pierce the dark.

Mary hid among the bushes in the garden of her grief,
While the gardener nursed the seedlings of new hope.
Till she recognized his presence and tore the veil apart,
Proclaiming resurrection as a liberating art.
She's a woman with a mission from now on,
Companions for empowerment will be won!
She defies the powers so sturdy, in her resurrected body.
The Wisdom Woman's radiance
Begets a fertile dawn.

Without these steadfast women standing first a distance off,
We never would have broken down the forces that exclude.
They broke into the realm where heart and spirit meet,
Excruciating agony with bitter hope so sweet.
They're the heart and soul of Christian faith,
Although their gifts we oft negate.
They defy the powers so sturdy, in the institution's body,
For you can't subdue the Risen one
In subverted female lore.

2. Resurrection Then

Mary:
Risen in our midst is the thrusting power of God,
The sun that shimmers through our gloom and fear.
Reverberating in the force-field of creation,
Disrupting all the powers of domination,
Mid the echoes of a frightening dislocation.
And something tells me it's a time for new engagement.
Far beyond the blood-stained hilltop,
There are victims who survive,
Unashamedly declaring
That the cross of shattered violence
Surrenders to the dawn.

Peter:
What the hell is she on to now?
Hysteria is a woman's greatest curse.
All this nonsense about rising from the dead,
Such crazy fantasizing in this hour of awful dread.
Reason and discretion we all need now instead,
Till proper leadership informs us the way to move ahead.
So, woman, cop yourself on,
Know your place and keep it.
Control that tongue of yours,
And let those who know the score
Lead us forth from here.

Mary:
Be not afraid — the words you often heard!
This strange and mighty paradox of hope released.
Turning all our cherished paradigms upside down,
Setting free the captives condemned to grieve and mourn,
A dangerous dream of liberation, a freedom newly born.
Peter, wake up, and face the echoes of a primal dawn.
Let go of the old rhetoric,
And the illusive lure of domination.
And let men and women forge together

The way of collaboration,
The dawn of a new dispensation.

Peter:
Mary, remember Eve, her arrogance and her pride.
The misbegotten species must learn to be wary.
We have had enough deluded Messiahs,
Abetted with false promises from Roman pariahs,
And importunate women trying to deny us
The God from high adorned in power and glory.
Surely descended from Abraham and Moses,
In the true line of holy men,
Who held their nerve and battles won.
Tradition is on our side,
Power alone will see us through.

Mary:
Peter, we have had the trophies and the triumphs,
Stained in the blood of those who died in vain.
Mutual empowerment is the only way through!
Companions for empowerment to relate anew,
An open table for every creature to imbue,
Where justice flourishes, oppression to undo.
Come on, Peter, the work awaits us,
The past is over and the dawn is here,
Victory goes before us and we, too,
Must follow the new way
To Galilee, where the Spirit leads beyond.

Peter:
You know too much for your own damn good.
Satan can quote Scripture as pleaseth him.
Delusion once again, I will not risk,
These messianic bidders, I will duly frisk.
My God, what I gave up, so willing and so brisk,
Alas for what! It was indeed a cruel deceptive trick
I'm going back fishing—I'll start afresh!
And this time, I will be in charge—be sure of that!

Mary:
Peter, from here on it is people you will catch.
Empowered and liberated in the lure of Risen truth.
Be open to the Spirit who will refresh
The broken reed within will no longer crush,
So embrace the wounded child with healing's touch.
You can do it, Peter, so get up and stretch,
And cast those tangled nets,
Deep into the primal seas,
No more just fish to catch
But God's world to explore,
The Risen Hope that shatters all before!

3. Resurrection Today!

So lay me down and let me sleep to slumber and to rest,
'Cause tomorrow is a special day for hope, for tears, for jest.
With my new heart and lungs replete, I'll rise to greet the dawn.
I'm homeward bound with my mum and dad on a happy Easter morn.

My hugs and kisses, I'll impart to surgeon, nurse, and staff,
And to Dr. Magdi Yacoub, who helped me once more laugh.
In a world of pain and anguish, where little children die,
The Harefield is a beacon of hope that I wish to hold up high.

Just weeks ago I stood aghast before an open grave,
But someone rolled away the stone, and God came forth to save.
The light shone in my darkness, and hope broke through my gloom,
As they rushed me for the transplant to the Harefield theater room.

An angel stood beside the tomb saying: "Do not be afraid,"
And do not weep or mourn; Christ has risen from the dead!
And goes before you all the way, as doctor, nurse, and friend.
The hope against all hopelessness is with you till the end.

He rose but once, we're often told, but that I do dispute,
'Cause I have seen God rise again when all seemed lost and mute.
We share a hope life can't defy; we are so richly blessed.
Thank God, its Easter morning, and I'm homeward bound at last!

4. Mrs. Cleopas Speaks!

We had this rare encounter as we journeyed toward Emmaus,
When a strange, familiar figure tagged along.
As my husband groaned and grumbled,
What he said was so much mumbled,
Confused and agitated by the things that had transpired.

He listened so intently to our sadness and our fears,
Our massive disappointment in the end.
For Israel's hoped redemption,
messianic intervention,
But it ended in disaster and broke my husband's heart.

The news about the empty tomb was baffling in extreme;
For my husband it was too much to take in.
And the bit he could not tolerate
Was the women trying to instigate
A story that the Savior had risen from the dead.

Then the guest began to explain how the whole lot was foretold;
I had said that to my husband many times.
Through the prophets right from Moses,
Ancient wisdom clearly shows us
That God is with the people in a promise now fulfilled.

But my husband couldn't take it in, a heart so full of doubt.
So the stranger led us to an upper room.
Bread and wine to reassure us,
Oft before it did secure us.
And the special guest had vanished as our eyes were opened wide.

This time he sure did get it — he somehow understood,
And asked if I had tablets to ease his burning heart.
He needed time to comprehend,
The broken heart will only mend
In bringing resurrection hope to a brokenhearted world.

For me, the road down to Emmaus evokes deep memories,
Confirming what I've known for many years.
Though the Gospel does not name me,
Some day they might reclaim me.
For without me—my dear Cleopas would never rise again!

5. Walking on Water

A long night rowing against the wind,
Their spirits down, their wits on end.
They wish he had been with them
Assuring with the power of wisdom.
Or the simple echo of enduring words:
"You must not be afraid."

They find a respite from rowing toil,
As sleepy eyes the senses do beguile.
And from their contemplating rest
They see the face that leads their quest.
The true but shocking revelation,
To calm their surging fears.

Some ghost-like figure on waters of a lake,
What is the Gospel truth that comes awake?
Empowered by faith in this encounter,
We touch a truth that's much profounder.
The enduring presence of the Risen One
Etched in every human gaze.

That mystical encounter we do not understand.
Whether walking on the water or threading nearby land.
That kind of breakthrough we're well aware,
Forever happening in our moments of despair.
That enduring presence of our living God
Comes very close indeed!

Chapter Fifteen

Empowerment
beneath the Language

*The true poem is the one where emotion has found the thought, and the thought
has found the words.* — ROBERT FROST

In the power of poetry, everything in creation has a voice with which to speak.
Even the silent stones carry resonances of ages past, and at some subtle level even
the stones know something of the underlying intelligence that keeps creation on
its course.

Geologian Thomas Berry consistently challenges us to embrace and include
everything that constitutes the living fabric of cosmic and planetary creation. He
writes: "Every component of the Earth community, both living and non-living,
has three rights: the right to be, the right to habitat or a place to be, and the right
to fulfill its role in the ever-renewing processes of the Earth community."[1]

It follows that everything that makes up the fabric of creation, including the
"nonliving," is entitled to a voice, to have its story told and its contribution ap-
preciated. The following set of poems are not the words of humans, but rather the
voices of the nonhuman arising from Gospel lore. If Jacob's well could speak what
might it say? Or the quiet mountain to which Jesus frequently escaped? Or even
the cross itself?

Poetry can release the inner voice and illuminate the inner substance. All the
more so as the objects and situations explored in these poems all contribute to the
archetypal awakening that gave birth once, and today continues to give birth, to
the *companionship of empowerment*.

◆ ◆ ◆

Poem 1: In our understanding of the parable of the sower (Mark 4:1–9; Matt.
13:1–9; Luke 8:4–8), we tend to moralize about different types of seeds and how
they might represent different stages of development — or lack of it — in our spir-
itual lives. We are in danger of forgetting the sheer miracle of seeds themselves —

182

irrespective of what ground they fall on. Among other things it has been noted that the energy field around a tiny seedling is the same as that of a fully grown plant or tree. Above all else a seed is a symbol of that fullness of life to which every living organism aspires. If more people were aware of this, then indeed we would be much more vigilant about how we scattered and planted the seeds.

Poem 2: Supposing Jacob's well (see John 4:5–42) itself could speak, what might it wish to say? And what further light might it throw on another amazing liberating and empowering Gospel story, where we see an empowered woman engaging Jesus in a highly symbolic theological conversation?[2]

Malina and Rohrbaugh make the following observation: The fact that the woman at the well is alone and that she comes at midday when the other village women are not there suggests that she has been shunned by the other women. She is perhaps seen as socially deviant (see 4:16–18).[3] She leaves her jar, indicating that she is not going home. Instead she goes to the public city square — where women were not supposed to go — as a disciple of new liberation![4]

Poem 3: "When we inquire into the meaning of the mountain," writes Pope Benedict XVI, "the mountain is the place of ascent — not only outward, but also inward ascent; it is a liberation from the burden of everyday life, a breathing in the pure air of creation; it offers a view of the broad expanse of creation and its beauty; it gives one an inner space to stand on and an intuitive sense of the Creator."[5]

Whether referring to Mount Sinai, Zion of Hebron, or perhaps some other, mountains symbolize throughout both the Old and New Testaments the meeting place between the earth and the heavenly realm. And Jesus frequently withdraws to a mountain (Matt. 4:25–8:1; 15:29–31; 17:1–8; 28:16–20), not just for personal refreshment but to ponder major issues requiring his attention, e.g., the choosing of the twelve. The mountain depicts a space for focusing attention and summoning the wisdom needed for the challenges that lie ahead.[6]

Poem 4: John P. Meier suggests that we should interpret the calming of the storm (Mark 4:35–41; Matt. 8:23–27; Luke 5:12–14) as a product of early Christian theology.[7] Again, we get some interesting insights in allowing the boat itself to speak. Instead of trying to figure out the supernatural power that might have been at work, in listening to the boat speak, we connect more deeply with the ordinary which tends to be a more reliable guide in breaking open the extraordinary nature of God's incarnation upon our earth. This helps to keep us more grounded in the companionship of empowerment.

Poem 5: We have already met the story of the widow's mite (Mark 12:41–44; Luke 21:1–4). This imaginative reconstruction imagines two small coins that may have meant a great deal to the widow, so loved and cherished by her that after she parted with them (in the temple) they somehow find their way right back into her possession again. Nature is full of strange anecdotes of this nature, perhaps a glimpse into a primordial wisdom that we, modern humans, have lost along life's journey.

Poem 6: If the cross could speak what might it say? We speak rather loosely of the cross as the tree of life, popularly believed to be a dogwood tree. In fact it is a tree cut down and lifeless now, used for violent life-destroying purposes that are totally alien to the nature of the tree understood botanically or archetypally.

In the religious consciousness of our species, the tree is a symbol of great age and wisdom. It is a primary symbol of the Great Earth Mother Goddess, the fruit-filled tree being an icon of her prodigious fertility. In all probability this is the symbolism of the tree in the Garden of Eden, quickly and brutally demonized by patriarchal interference, when set up a fundamental sense of disharmony for which the primordial female is blamed. In fact, the real culprit is the interfering male. In the book of Genesis, the tree is not respected and neither is the one who engages fruitfully with the tree, namely, the woman.

The tree continues to be crucified in our contemporary world, as tropical forests are ravaged, and excessive logging adversely affects the well-being of earth and person alike. The rich eco-systemic significance of trees, while scientifically well established, is poorly understood by the public generally and particularly by those for whom greedy consumerism is their primary value. We have certainly inherited a crucifixion of the tree; surely the time has come for a resurrection of the tree!

Poem 7: Pinching wheat on the Sabbath (Mark 2:23–28; Matt. 12:1–8; Luke 6:1–5): what a wonderful incarnational story this is — full of playful, teasing human tenderness (despite a confused use of Old Testament texts). And the setting of the Sabbath day indicates that even childlike behavior can take on prophetic meaning in the face of institutional intransigence.

There is a kind of frivolous tenor to this story, pinching somebody else's wheat and having a nibble, knowing that the powers-that-be will notice and that it will really irritate them. Yet the message is deadly serious. A new empowerment is being born — proclaim it by fair means or foul, but keep it humorous. Humor is a survival strategy when you take on the powers of oppression, especially the religious ones.

1. Sprouting Voices

The problem with us little seedlings,
We flourish so gracious and great.
And the sower tends to scatter us widely
So at times we cannot cultivate.
We fall on the pathways and brambles
And we're scattered on stony ground too.
And despite the adverse predilections,
We sprout and give life to the new.

We seedlings that fall on the pathway,
For the birds we're easy to consume.
While the stones interfere with our rooting
And we roast by the heat of the noon.
And our friends called the thistles and thorns
Are stronger by far in their power.
We're really designed for the good soil
Where we flourish and grow by the hour.

Now Matthew said strange things about us
Suggesting we signify much.
We little ones choked by the thorns
Resemble the greed of the rich.
While our stony existence if fleeting
Like those who are lacking in depth.
For the ones that fall on the pathway
Understanding is often inept.

However, we're given the credit
So fertile and fruitful are we.
In the soul of the earth ever ready
We'll flourish and sprout faithfully.
And the Gospel compares us to people
Abundantly fruitful endowed.
So together we'll relish creation,
A venture that makes us all proud.

2. Jacob's Well

From thirsting earth and luscious spring, they carved my pregnant womb,
Where gushing waters ebb and flow,
To pacify each thirsting soul.
I am the proud wellspring inebriating life and hope.

Yes, I remember well the day he sat upon my lap.
His inner soul was parched,
His body pained and wearied.
And he longed for living water to spring up within his soul.

And from Samaria, there came a woman with a jug.
The eyes of strangers meet astride;
Strained feelings rise and then subside.
"Please give me living water from your jug-like womb of life."

Boundaries are transgressed and many rules are broken,
As they share a common vessel,
And build bridges new to wrestle,
With all the broken hopes of outdated make-believe.

She talked about the silted streams of five painful reigns.
She thirsted for new life,
Weary of all the power and strife.
And she knew he was a kindred soul of liberating grace.

She left the jug behind, a memorial for ages hence;
And to her town-folks she ran in zest,
With eager wellsprings to behest!
A New Reign now unleashed, unimagined freedom and fresh hope.

They came in droves, embracing holy space of Jacob fame.
It filled my heart with joy.
And with pregnant tears I sighed:
"Come to my waters, friends; this well will never dry!"

3. The Discerning Mountain Space

I came forth from an explosion, volcanic from within.
I rise above the valley plains,
To kiss the sun and greet the rains,
The meeting place for mystery, symbolic to the core.

In the Scriptures of the Hebrews, I hold an honored place.
The site where God is manifest,
A sacred space from all the rest.
Folks like Moses and Elijah approach in holy dread.

In the Gospel of St. Matthew I illuminate the plot.
Whether Sinai, Zion, or Hebron,
With disciples or with no one,
Jesus oft invokes my guiding light his mission to fulfill.

From my source of holy wisdom, discernment unfolds.
I'm the mount of initiation,
Of transfigured transformation,
I empower the source of healing in disciples I send forth.

Jesus oft invoked my wisdom in the silence of my heights.
Weighed down by so much friction,
He embraced a bigger vision,
And regained some fresh perspective for the valleys down below.

Long before the Christian story and long after it's been told,
The liminal invades our human space,
Keeping balance and fidelity in place,
Seeing more clearly when the vision is enlarged.

The space of liminality invites each seeking soul.
Come apart when life is crowded,
And your spirit deep is troubled,
And drink afresh of wisdom for the road that lies ahead.

4. I'm the Boat in Which He Slept!

I remember well that day!
He sat on my stern seat,
And addressed the crowds in parables:
The farmer and the seeds he scattered,
The mustard seed, though small, it mattered,
The word will glow like light imparted!
And all the while, my body swayed
To the gentle rhythm of his stirring words,
In the restful waters of the Sea of Galilee.

I was glad to hear the echo of his words,
That I should sail across the lake
To greet the setting sun.
Far out from shore the wind arose
While whipping waves in storm blows,
And scared disciples in fear they froze.
While he who knew too well the storms of daily life,
Rested his brow on stern-head secure,
Impervious to the frantic fears of reluctant seafarers.

I knew those waters all too well!
And so did he — having accompanied the fishing fleets
through many ups and downs.
They wake him from his resting slumber,
Electrified by gale and thunder,
Feels like their whole world might fall asunder.
Till his reassuring words
Calm the insecurities of their troubled souls,
And the choppy waters no longer haunt their fear.

For me, this had been a long day!
And I looked forward to berthing down
In my old familiar docking space.
Till shrieking screams of the demonic
Rippled through the waters in pained harmonic,
From out the tombs so dreary and catatonic.
As pigs rushed down, one landed

On my vessel's stern-head,
And water splashed as if another storm brewed
While the brokenhearted cry out in messianic hope.

Sometime, late that night,
I heard footsteps crawl across my brow.
Home at last, a wearied body lay down to rest.
Safely, we had reached the final shore,
Beyond the storms we long endure.
Good night, my special guest. I hope you rest secure!

5. Mighty Little Mites

Minted together and packaged as one,
and banked in the same institution.
Together we landed in a small baker shop,
till the day when a widow some cookies she bought.
As small change we became her possession.

We had left the domain of anonymous coins
and the banter of consuming indulgence.
The widow she cherished each coin she possessed;
we were counted and checked with the greatest respect.
We were gifted with loving attention.

From her handful of coins we were chosen aloft.
We felt nervous but we trusted the widow.
And together we served as an offering to God,
in a temple where money defines every word.
We felt lost but at least were together.

The high priests at night took stock of the store.
They checked all the big stuff leaving us on the floor.
Brushed into a bucket designed for the poor,
Our future precarious, scared and unsure.
But, at least, we still had each other.

And Stephen the deacon, God bless his kind heart,
Took us to Broadway where poor folks consort.

And together we happened to be in his grasp,
As he handed us over, we were gratefully clasped.
Not sure where the vendor would take us.

And then came the shock and surprise of a life.
The wisdom of providence does strange things at times.
On a ledge where a handful was regularly kept,
And a wrinkled soft hand would frequently check.
'Twas the treasured domain of the widow.

Since then we have traveled through many a space,
And fortune diverted our journeys.
But we each oft recall with grateful delight
How God chose us both to be the widow's mite.
To inspire giving hearts for all nations.

6. When the Cross Speaks

Why they cut me down I will never understand!
A sprouting cypress, thirty years and three,
So fertile, elegant, and free.
I was in my prime,
As luscious and flourishing as nature could design.
Why they cut me down I will never understand.

Did they know my ancient heritage aloft?
Representing no one less
Than the one-time Great Goddess,
Whose leaves and foliage,
Under heaven embraced a tradition of great age.
Why they cut me down I will never understand.

And that crude cross emasculated from my trunk,
With Jesus executed,
A prophet brave reputed.
He, too, was in the prime of life,
Whose mission sought to end all strife.
Why they cut HIM down, I will never understand.

Today, one thousand Filipinos died.
No trees to halt the sliding mud,
It wrecked their homes and left them dead.
A mountainside so bare,
By corporations who show no love nor care.
Why they cut them down, I will never understand.

They say the cross redeems and offers hope.
I have to disagree,
There's no life in a dead tree!
Religion's contradiction,
So much reckless pain and widespread friction.
Cut down that bloody cross and supplant it with a tree.

7. Pinching Wheat on the Sabbath

The birds of the air can munch as they like,
And will do so when they're feeling hungry.
And I and my followers said we'd do the same
To celebrate nature's own grandeur.
The farmer won't mind if we pinch from his wheat
In the midst of abundant creation.
He too will sample from some other one's lot
A Sabbath of rich fermentation.

But legalists watching were shocked to the core
Breaking laws they had stupidly crafted.
Forgetting that David in ages long past
Had devoured bread reserved for the fathers.
And who observes Sabbath in minute detail?
Even priests can't observe regulations.
Like the wheat that we pinch, we treat the law light
And embrace the Sabbath celebrations.

I'm seeking for mercy and not sacrifice
Declaring a new dispensation.
The wheat that we pluck will quickly replete,

Abundant in God's great creation.
The Sabbath is holy for wholesome release,
Round the table where everyone's welcome.
And never submit to Sabbatical rules
For the Sabbath is there for the human.

Chapter Sixteen

Empowerment through Human Solidarity

It may be said that we inherited poetry from the universe. Creation was set in form and framed in rhythm long before mankind became part of it.

— LOUIS UNTERMEYER

More than anything else, Christian faith is about empowerment. What Christians celebrate in the historical event of Jesus of Nazareth is a specific appropriation of divine incarnation active from the dawn of time, and in humans ever since we first evolved seven million years ago.

In conventional Christian thought, "Incarnation" pertains only to the historical Jesus with reference solely to human beings. I suggest we expand the meaning in two directions, first that Incarnation is about God's immersion in and identity with bodies—all bodies, from that of the cosmos to the basic bacteria of organic life. In other words, God loves bodies and through the medium of the body God incarnates throughout all of creation.

Second, in reference to the human, God has incarnated in the human since we first began to evolve seven million years ago. God has always been with us in the fullness of incarnational empowerment—from the very beginning. Throughout our long human story there surely have been times when the divine became more explicitly incarnate, affirming and supporting what was transpiring in our evolution at those critical junctures. The most recent of such moments was the axial age occurring about two thousand years ago. For Christians, Jesus is the distinctive incarnation of God for that transitional time.

Axial ages, however, as highlighted by Karen Armstrong, are not for one sector of humanity, but for all humans.[1] Therefore, we can expect such incarnational affirmations in other spheres of human culture as well. Once we make this connection some of the other manifestations become all too obvious: the avatars of Hinduism,[2] the bodhisattvas of Buddhism, the prophets of Islam, the diviners of indigenous African religions, the shamans (and shamanesses) of prehistoric times.[3]

In all cases, we are dealing with human beings, but so highly developed that they serve as incarnations of the divine, inspiring empowering models for the rest of us to emulate. Limiting incarnation to the Christian Jesus undermines the grandeur of God not merely in other religions but also in Christianity itself.

◆ ◆ ◆

The poems of this section attempt to highlight the aftermath of the life, death, and resurrection of Jesus. How are Christians meant to embrace the liberation and empowerment of the primordial story and live it out? Christendom has reserved that task to the body of believers known as *the church*. But, today, many have lost faith in the church, and Christian faith is rapidly outgrowing its traditional institutional structures.

A new ferment is at work, creating a fluidity, creativity, and chaos that the guardians of major institutions distinctly dislike. It feels so threatening! And, indeed, it is — but also full of hope and promise. Millions who are no longer formal Christians, or perhaps never were, are meeting Jesus afresh as an inspiring and empowering figure. Millions of lay people study theology and spirituality. Faith has broken out of the institution and is being broken open by a newly emerging generation of spiritual seekers.

The poet wishes to include and cherish all these people — just as Jesus would! For the poet, these are precisely the people who seek and search, struggle and dream alternatives; these are the very ones who provide grist for the mill of life, guardians of the dangerous memory, the fiery ferment from which all poetry — and new possibility — is born.

The two-thousand-year tradition has a limited relevance in the rapidly evolving world of our time. Like all the other religions, however, Christianity is endowed with archetypal truths, and these endure across time and culture. It is these deeper truths that occupy the poetic imagination. How these truths translate into the emerging culture of our time is what the poems of this final section seek to articulate.

Poem 1: A Christianity for the future that seeks to be relevant, liberating, and empowering must give priority to the land itself, as God's primary gift. The land is a foundational expression of incarnational embodiment; in a sense it is the primordial expression of God's revealing truth, where God was revealing God's self for billions of years before humanity or the religions ever evolved. Several scholars cited in this work (e.g., William R. Herzog II, Richard Horsley, Bruce J. Malina) claim that for the Hebrew people, the land is God's primary covenantal gift, and that it carries the same depth of meaning for Jesus in his life and ministry.

When writing the Gospels, had the evangelists themselves already lost sight of this fact? If the land, and justice for the land, are so central in the bedrock Hebrew tradition, why do the Gospel writers pay so little attention to the subject? Might it be that the more heady preoccupations of Greek metaphysics led to a disconnect from the groundedness of all living reality? So preoccupied with getting it right in the head, we neglected the body, both that of the earth and the human.

We will probably never succeed in getting a comprehensive answer to these questions. Meanwhile, there is little doubt that a contemporary Jesus would highlight and prioritize the urgent earth questions of our time. And that is what the poet seeks to honor in the opening poem of this section, created around the time cycle of each day.

Poem 2: In a previous work I detailed the fascinating research of contemporary paleoanthropologists, uncovering our human origins, now dating back seven million years.[4] This affects not merely our self-understanding, but also how Christians define and articulate the notion of Incarnation. For God, it was fundamentally good, from the very beginning, and that is what the poet seeks to captivate in this poem.

Poem 3: It is not by accident, I suggest, that each parable opens with the word: *Imagine* ... people going to sow seeds ... going to a wedding feast ..., workers in the vineyard, etc. Jesus was enthralled with a new dream, a vision of a different Israel, an alternative world in which the powerless would be empowered to live in a new way with each other, with the earth, and with their God.

The liberation theologian Gustavo Gutiérrez has said that one may rob the poor of many things, but one cannot rob them of their imagination. So, perhaps, despite the cultural conditioning, Jesus knew that he could reawaken imagination, even in the most resistant, some of whom were his own disciples. Imagination is a Christian virtue we must always safeguard with the creative mind of the poet.

Poem 4: Christian theologians — fiercely at times — reserve the notion of incarnation solely to Christian faith. As indicated in the general introduction to this chapter, such an exclusive claim seriously undermines the Gospel values of inclusiveness and mutual empowerment. What we have in common with the other great religions, and the older spiritual traditions, is far more significant than how we differ from each other. As a species, we have so much more to gain by highlighting commonalities rather than differences.

Christians need to forgo the inherited arrogance and divisive superiority and allow the freedom and subversive vision of the poet to co-create an alternative pathway to affirm and celebrate the richness of our cultural and religious diversity.

Poem 5: Here the poet picks up the missionary theme of the Christian faith: Go make disciples of all nations. The reference to the 153 species of fish in the sea (see John 21:11) is a much debated text, with some commentators noting the possible underlying mathematical symbolism. In the time of Pythagoras, 153 was most significant for being one of the two numbers in the closest fraction known, at the time, to the true value of the square root of 3, the fraction in question being 265/153 (the difference between this and the square root of 3 is merely 0.000025). The ratio of 153:265 was consequently known throughout the Hellenic world as "the measure of the fish." Not surprising, therefore, that Jerome, claimed that the Greeks had identified that there were exactly 153 species of fish in the sea.

It seems like this was the best device available to the writer to describe a very large number. There is nothing here to justify Christian missionaries conquering everything and everybody for Christ, an interpretation whereby the Christian missionary effort in the nineteenth and twentieth centuries became enmeshed in the forces of Western colonialism. Today, the missionary endeavor strives to be much more dialogical, mutually empowering, and committed to the integrity of creation; how this translates into practical action varies enormously throughout the Christian world. Missiology today is very much a discipline in transition.

Poem 6: The story of the Ascension is recorded in Luke 24:50–51 and in Acts 1:9–11. As indicated by Marcus J. Borg,[5] cosmology seems to be the crucial issue here. In New Testament times, the universe was perceived in a three-tier system: the heavens above, Hades (hell) beneath, and the earth in between. That seems to be the popular awareness of our time too. The Ascension is probably best understood as a story invented to get Jesus back to heaven after the Resurrection.

In our time we can understand it as a metaphorical statement of God's radical presence in the whole of creation. By "ascending" Jesus enters into the full scope of all creation as understood in contemporary cosmology, the one universal creation devoid of all our man-made hierarchical tiers and dualistic divisions.

Poem 7: This poem picks up Teilhard de Chardin's pregnant insight that our biological evolution as a human species is close to completion; biologically, we can't evolve much further. That being the case we are now at a new evolutionary threshold, invited to embrace a future in which *psychic evolution* (mind and spirit) will be to the fore.

Is the Resurrected Jesus a foretaste of what that might mean for all of us? The poet certainly wants to run with that idea, envisaging Jesus, not as an interventionist seeking to correct some fundamental flaw, but rather as the one who affirms and confirms all we have achieved over the seven million years of our evolution, and points the way forward to our next major evolutionary stage. Jesus may be understood as a kind of bridge-builder, helping us to see the connecting threads between our deep past and the future that lures us on.[6]

Poem 8: The parting word — Jesus bids adieu! However, it is a farewell that honors fully the companionship of empowerment. Jesus goes before us, a model to inspire and challenge, but never so much beyond our reach as to leave us feeling unworthy, confused, and certainly not abandoned. Jesus remains with us the whole way, never in a patronizing role, but always in the proactive creativity and liberating empowerment, that seeks to call forth the adult in every person.

To the contrary, the plethora of Christian denominations that populate the contemporary world seem to invest an enormous amount of money, power, and arrogance trying to keep people in a kind of dysfunctional subservience to a Jesus they often portray as a ruling king from thousands of miles away. The monopolizing cult of the temple priesthood still comes between us and the Jesus who is radically present where the few, or many, gather to celebrate incarnation — in every endeavor that is about birthing forth the companionship of empowerment.

1. Grounded in the Land

A fresh dawn awakens the luster and lush,
The landscape so urgently fertile.
So sensual the dew for the animal taste,
Awakening eyes for bacterial haste.
Reweaving the Spirit's outpouring.

The forenoon calls forth the farmer with seed,
The vineyard adorns new vintage.
And sunlight bestows the gift of all time,
Photosynthesizing in nature's great rhyme.
While shepherd and sheep graze new pasture.

At midday, the fruit of the earth is aglow,
While the mustard seed aches in fermenting.
And tiny seeds sprout into planting array,

While the birds in the branches indulge in such play.
And life is abundantly fruitful.

At evening the Spirit is restful and calm,
The fields and their lilies are joyful.
The deep sense of relish atouching the soil,
While beauty and pain embrace human toil.
The land is God's gift to the human.

In the darkness of night, fertility thrives,
In the mating and bonding erotic.
The Jubilee rest restores the true cost,
To regenerate the spent and the lost.
The cycle of grace and becoming.

The earth is imbued with a power to renew,
The breadth and the fire of the Spirit.
Long before the human did ever evolve,
God's earthly embrace was the heart of true love.
Be at home in the earth and its beauty.

2. Enfleshing the Human Anew (Incarnation Reclaimed)

I was there when the Bonobos swept the world by surprise,
With their matriarchal fondness and their keen erotic bias.
I was there when evolution pushed the primates further on,
And humans first unfolded, incarnational so grand!
Make no mistake about it, I was there!

In the holy land of Africa, the human first came forth
And flourished with great elegance in tribes of every sort.
I was there when you descended from the trees to fertile soil
And relished every moment of your childlike, playful wile.
Make no mistake about it, I was there!

I was there when you built water rafts to sail the mighty seas
And I watched in real amazement when the flame from flint you teased.

I was there when you were dancing in your worship and your prayer.
I admired your love for nature and your tendency to care.
Make no mistake about it, I was there!

I was there when the Neanderthals mastered skills with rock and bone.
I befriended Homo Sapiens, wisdom previously unknown.
I was there when human language, a mighty skill evolved,
And delighted in the artists and the images they carved.
Make no mistake about it, I was there!

Seven million years evolving, I witnessed every day,
To the threshold of maturity the heavens would declare.
And the Jesus affirmation at the sacred hour of time,
A remarkable celebration of a species so sublime.
Make no mistake about it, I was there!

And other incarnations erupted round the globe
To mark the sacred breakthrough, all humankind unfold.
You never got it perfect but I can work with that,
You have done as well as any species, a brilliant work of art.
Make no mistake about it, I was there!

From this apex of achievement, you evolve a stage along.
Beyond the biological, the psychic beckons on.
In my resurrected presence, with the Spirit to imbue,
You're blessed with the resources to see the whole thing through.
And make no mistake about it, I'll be there!

3. Disciples with Imagination

There's no looking back when you're faced with a task
To imagine the lure of the future.
The structures of old, ruling God from on high,
Bless our time with another departure.
We need to imagine a future so new,
Transcending the laws of religion.
The Spirit now echoes another refrain:
Imagine... Imagine... Imagine!

Imagine a farmer with seeds that can sprout
A harvest of God's liberation.
Imagine a wedding with much wine afloat
Athirst for a new celebration.
Imagine a woman abirthing the bread
In a world of rife malnutrition.
Betray not the call of the Gospel refrain:
Imagine . . . Imagine . . . Imagine!

Imagine the crippled, the blind, and the lame,
Set free from the bondage of guilt.
Imagine dispelling demonic disease,
The anguish that millions have felt.
Imagine the vineyard where justice prevails
With dignified work once again.
Oppression derailed by a different refrain:
Imagine . . . Imagine . . . Imagine!

Imagine a Kingdom with no king at all,
Co-dependent relations undone.
Imagine empowerment embraced mutually,
The grace and the freedom we've won.
Imagine the hope that baffles despair,
Uplifting the millions condemned.
More joy on the earth to sing the refrain:
Imagine . . . Imagine . . . Imagine!

Imagine a world where war is no more,
Nonviolence will break through at last.
Beyond the resentment and grudges we hold,
And the war games so brutally cast.
Imagine a planet where all feel at home,
The blessing of God's re-creation.
I make all things new — forever proclaim:
Imagine . . . Imagine . . . Imagine!

4. In Solidarity with Other Incarnations

An axial age it certainly was,
Evolution was poised at a threshold.
A critical time the human awaits,
Embracing the psychic is raising the stakes,
The Spirit rejoices and congratulates,
The breakthrough is happening all over!

The West lauds its heroes and Jesus became
Exclusively bodied incarnate.
The empowering companion was largely ignored,
A king-like Messiah was given the role,
Too often depicted in European lore,
As the one who would rescue all nations.

Meanwhile, in the East, the Spirit awakes
Avatars in the Hindu tradition.
While Buddhism claims that bodhisattvas,
Embodying a fullness that never withdraws,
Divine radiation to the human it calls,
The breakthrough is happening all over.

The Muslims as well have figures imbued
With a fullness of God-like adorn.
They call them the Prophets to lure and inspire,
Inclusive of Jesus and Mary beside,
To serve us as models we always devise,
The breakthrough is happening all over.

The Diviner of Africa will hold a place too,
With Shamans across many cultures.
The axial age impinges on all,
Incarnating goodness and power to install,
Transitioning forward for nothing can stall,
The breakthrough is happening all over.

Please spare me embarrassment too long endured,
Imposed upon all other peoples.
As if I alone could save from their plight,

Projected aloft with divine power and might,
While the ground incarnation we miss the insight
that the breakthrough is happening all over.

5. To the Nations and Beyond

It's a parabolic number to depict a distant scene,
The horizon that invigorates new life.
A reminder that the vision for which Jesus lived and died,
Stretches all the false distinctions we devise.
We're disciples with the fishing nets we forever haul ashore,
The fruitfulness our mission to empower.
And we do it as companions with every tribe and race,
Ever wary of the greed that could devour.

Our missionary story has often been endowed
With echoes too colonial by far.
And the faith that we've imparted with arrogance attached,
Has oft been used to serve a holy war.
We have imposed on others an ideology
As if we alone were bearers of the truth.
And desecrated wisdom, indigenous and rich,
Playing power games with the Gospel in pursuit.

The missionary endeavor must carve another route,
In justice for all peoples and the earth.
Collaborating partnerships to build a better world
Is the mandate of the Gospel in its heart.
The image of the fishing nets, the fullness of the catch,
Exemplifies diversity so wide.
We weave the web together in holiness and truth,
And gently sail the Spirit's rising tide.

6. Ascension: Taken Up to Embrace All

Cosmology can be misleading
When we picture the world too small.
And impose all the layers of dominion,
Entrapped in a power to enthrall.
I could not ascend into heaven
'Cause heaven is right here on earth.
Rather lifting within the creation,
I celebrate God's cosmic birth.

Ascension is really descending,
Embracing the fullness of life.
Acclaiming God's flourishing wisdom
Mid the journey of struggle and strife.
The clouds in the sky have their beauty
Dispensing the waters of life.
And you'll find me right there in the water,
The Spirit who flows in each tide.

So stop looking up to the heavens,
In search of a God high above.
Look into the eye of the other
And spare not your efforts to love.
Include in that gaze the creation,
The place where you flourish and grow.
And divide not this beautiful cosmos
Where there's neither above nor below.

7. The Psychic Future

I never came to intervene; I came to celebrate.
Affirming and confirming what humans had achieved.
Across emerging aeons fulfilling ancient hope,
Embodying incarnation so elegant in scope.
You never got it fully right but I can live with that,
You co-created freely and bravely played your part.

And now we've reached the moment adieu I bid you all,
Transcending the embodied to heed the Spirit's call.
The Spirit now will lead you forth, a moment new indeed,
For evolution's forward thrust in every thought and deed.
Beyond the biological, adventure to fulfill,
The psychic is the realm new in God's creative skill.
So leave behind the fishing nets and comforts you have known,
And stand before the universe embracing God's new dawn!

8. I Go before You . . . but Never beyond You!

I go before you always,
Yet you are my body, the voice of my hope,
The deep Incarnation, to light every nation,
A mission embracing incredible scope.

I go before you always,
But without you the dream will never unlock
The reign of empowerment, a mutual endowment,
A new dawn for freedom that time will not stop.

I go before you always,
Where two or three gather in the power of my name,
Disciples are equal, keep all structures supple,
Set free all from bondage, afire in new flame.

I go before you always,
I will never forsake you, affirming your truth,
Together we'll do it, empowered to pursue it,
God's new re-creation, is sure to bear fruit.

Epilogue

Jesus, the Androgyne

According to Aristotle, biology defines human identity, constituting us as male or female. And for Aristotle, real identity is with the male. *Androgyny,* on the other hand, defines an unfolding state of psychic integration deeming biologically defined identity to be of secondary importance. In our contemporary culture, two quite distinctive issues of androgyny and sexual orientation are often confused.

For the androgyne, the biological identity of being male or female is not under question or attack. There is no quibble about one's biological identity. The androgyne experiences life differently, drawn toward a deeper integration that is of *psychic* rather than *biological* significance.[1] In this inner journey, the biological distinctions between male and female lose much of their absolute, dualistic clarity. The androgyne forever yearns for a deeper union, which transcends, but does not seek to eliminate, the biological distinctions. In fact, on the androgynous journey, the person becomes more enriched, complex, and fulfilled as a male or a female.

In the androgyne, the focus shifts from external determinants and moves toward inner growth, greater spiritual depth, and psychic integration. In the contemporary world, which prioritizes dualistic divisions, clinical clarity, rational analysis, and patriarchal control (all features of Aristotelian philosophy), negotiating the androgynous journey is not easy. Yet many people go through this experience, one that is rarely named or acknowledged, never mind affirmed, in the confused world of our time.

As an archetype of the truly human, in all probability, Jesus was an androgyne,[2] and that insight has particular appeal to the poet. It is often suggested that other great religious leaders, e.g., Buddha, Krishna, and certain shamans, were also androgynous. In the true spirit of poetic transparency, the poet wants to hear out the androgynous Jesus, who as an androgyne can authentically claim to be all things to all people, and particularly to the many women persecuted, oppressed, and excluded in the name of Jesus — who for much of Christendom has been ideologically defined and deified as a biological male.

Let's dismantle the edifice that vouches for the truth.
Let's discard the neat distinctions Aristotle once approved.
Let's demolish the monopoly of patriarchal lore
And untangle the distortions that served us heretofore.

    CHORUS:
    Let light shine — to illuminate a landscape,
    Buried deep beneath the rubble,
    The useful fabrications of outdated make-believe!

Let's embrace a deeper wisdom that can truly celebrate
The complexity of nature and the greatness of our state.
In the archetypal human I embrace what you divide,
The masculine and feminine forever intertwine. CHORUS.

Let's embark upon a pilgrimage which ancient sages knew,
Beyond the biological, the psychic will imbue.
A deeper integration where male and female meet,
Androgynous identity makes everyone complete. CHORUS.

I represent a fullness, God's holy life to lead,
Transcending the distortions of the propagating seed.
Defining our biology, determining a truth,
Perversely undermining the psyche's deeper root. CHORUS.

The human in its greatness cannot be quantified.
The truth of our identity erupts from deep inside,
A fundamental unity defines our every goal,
The mystery of our oneness embellishes the soul. CHORUS.

Conclusion

Poetry ... will never finally solve anything because it is the voice of new promise, the art of permanent beginning. ——BRENDAN KENNELLY

It is my contention that the issue of power/empowerment will be the greatest challenge of the next hundred years. We have learned for so long that the power lies elsewhere; thus it will be a hard task to recover the divine dignity, passion, and power that are ours by birth. ——LISA ISHERWOOD

Notes

Introduction

1. See Chatwin, *Songlines*.

Chapter One / It Happened Like This

1. O'Murchu, *Catching Up with Jesus*.
2. Housden, *Ten Poems to Change Your Life*, 4.
3. Douglas-Klotz, *The Hidden Gospel*.

Chapter Two / Poetry Unlocks Deeper Meaning

1. Fiand, *From Religion Back to Faith*; Harris, *The End of Faith*.
2. See Wallace, *Hidden Dimensions*.
3. Hillman, *Archetypal Psychology*.
4. Brown, *The Da Vinci Code*.
5. Harpur, *The Pagan Christ*.
6. Wink, *The Human Being*.
7. See O'Murchu, *Ancestral Grace*.
8. Moule, "The Meaning of 'Life' in the Gospels and Epistles of St. John."
9. Sheehan, *The First Coming*, 67.

Chapter Three / Poetry and the Story of Jesus

1. Perrin, *Jesus and the Language of the Kingdom*.
2. Wright, *Jesus and the Victory of God*.
3. Song, *Jesus and the Reign of God*, 162.
4. Ogden, *On Theology*, 43.
5. Useful notes can be found in Douglas-Klotz, *The Hidden Gospel*. See also *www.abwoon.com/news.html*.
6. Sheehan, *The First Coming*; *www.infidels.org/library/modern/thomas_sheehan/firstcoming/bibliography.html*.
7. E.g., Crossan, *God and Empire*; Horsley, *Jesus and Empire*; Schüssler Fiorenza, *In Memory of Her*.
8. Fuellenbach, *The Kingdom of God*.
9. In Borg, *Jesus at 2000*, 22–55.
10. Dunn, *Christianity in the Making*, 610–11.

Chapter Four / Empowerment beyond the Lure of Kingship

1. See *www.lifeofchrist.com/life/genealogy/print.html.*
2. Wink, *The Human Being,* 250.
3. Spencer, *What Did Jesus Do?* 150.
4. For further information, see Howard-Brook and Gwyther, *Unveiling Empire.*
5. See Crossan, *God and Empire.*

Chapter Five / How God Gives Birth to Empowerment

1. Fox, *One River, Many Wells,* 41.
2. Jantzen, *Becoming Divine.*
3. See Johnson, *Truly Our Sister.*
4. See Reid-Bowen, *Goddess as Nature.*
5. Schaberg, *Illegitimacy of Jesus,* and Lüdemann, *Virgin Birth?*
6. Spencer, *What Did Jesus Do?* 199n.16.
7. Coffey, *Hidden Women of the Gospels,* 17–25.
8. Telford, "The Barren Temple and the Withered Tree."
9. Johnson, *She Who Is*; Schüssler Fiorenza, *Jesus: Miriam's Child, Sophia's Prophet*; Edwards, *Jesus, the Wisdom of God*; Witherington, *Jesus the Sage.*

Chapter Six / Hidden Years to Awaken Empowerment

1. See Harvey, *Son of Man,* 26–31.
2. *Aquarian Gospel*, written by John F. Sullivan and produced by William Keenan; much of the information in this movie is based on the book by Holger Kersten, *Jesus Lived in India* (2001).
3. See Harvey, *Son of Man,* 87–128.
4. See Bauckham, *Gospel Women,* 98–99.
5. For further elucidation, see Barclay and Drane, *The Gospel of Matthew.*
6. See valuable notes at *www.biblicalhebrew.com/nt/lovehate.htm.*

Chapter Seven / Empowering the Disempowered: Healing

1. See Crossan, *The Historical Jesus,* 303–32; Malina and Rohrbaugh, *Social Science Commentary on the Gospel of John,* 114ff.
2. Pilch, *Healing in the New Testament,* 76.
3. Davies, *Jesus the Healer;* Montefiore, *The Miracles of Jesus.*
4. Wiebe, *God and Other Spirits.*
5. Myers, *Binding the Strong Man,* 154–55.
6. Myers, *Binding the Strong Man,* 192.
7. For valuable background information on the political-symbolic context of this story, see Horsley, *Jesus and Empire,* 98–103; Wright, *Jesus and the Victory of God,* 502–7; Myers, *Binding the Strong Man,* 190–94.
8. Heim, *Saved from Sacrifice,* 150ff.
9. Herzog, *Prophet and Teacher,* 85.
10. Marshall, *Beyond Retribution,* 173.

11. See the commentary by Dr. Ralph F. Wilson at *www.Jesuswalk.com/lessons/13_10-17.htm*.

12. See *www.noetic.org/research/dh/main.html*; see also *www.stephanaschwartz.com/distant_healing_biblio.htm*.

Chapter Eight / Empowering the Disempowered: Storytelling

1. See Julicher's seminal work, *Die Gleichnisreden Jesu*, 2 vols. (1888–99).

2. E.g., Crossan, *In Parables*; Herzog, *Parables as Subversive Speech*; Hedrick, *Many Things in Parables*; Schottroff, *The Parables of Jesus*.

3. Herzog, *Parables as Subversive Speech*; *Prophet and Teacher*.

4. See Herzog, *Parables as Subversive Speech*, Myers, *Binding the Strong Man*; Schottroff, *The Parables of Jesus*, 223.

5. Herzog, *Parables as Subversive Speech*, 240ff.

6. Horsley, *Jesus and Empire*, 53.

7. See Schottroff, *The Parables of Jesus*, 210ff.

8. Herzog, *Parables as Subversive Speech*, 94.

9. Kloppenborg, *The Tenants in the Vineyard*.

10. Schottroff, *The Parables of Jesus*, 101.

11. Further elucidation in Rosenblatt, "Got into the Party After All."

12. See Borg, *Meeting Jesus Again for the First Time*, 50ff.

13. Reiser, *Jesus and Judgment*.

14. See Lee, *Flesh and Glory*, 125.

15. See *www.hoshanarabbah.org/pdfs/heb_grk.pdf*.

Chapter Nine / Empowering the Disempowered: Radical Inclusiveness

1. Crossan, *The Historical Jesus*, 341–44.

2. Spencer, *What Did Jesus Do?* 59.

3. Karris, *Luke: Artist and Theologian*, 47.

4. Lee, *Flesh and Glory*.

5. Groody, *Globalization, Spirituality, and Justice*, 50.

6. Schimmel, *Wounds Not Healed by Time*.

7. Wink, *The Powers That Be*, 171.

8. See Herzog, *Parables as Subversive Speech*, 182ff.; Klawans, "Moral and Ritual Purity."

Chapter Ten / Empowered to Relate Nonviolently

1. Brandon, *Jesus and the Zealots*.

2. Wink, *Naming the Powers*; *Unmasking the Powers*; *Engaging the Powers*; *The Powers That Be*; Dear, *www.JohnDear.org*; Rynne, *Gandhi and Jesus*.

3. Wink, *The Powers That Be*, 121.

4. See *www.nonviolenceworks.com; www.rainonline.org*.

5. Wink, *The Powers That Be*, 101ff.

6. See Harvey, *Son of Man*, 44–55.

7. Sheehan, *Jesus and the Zealots*, 68.

8. Malina and Rohrbaugh, *Social Science Commentary on the Gospel of John,* 77–78.

9. In Levine, *The Historical Jesus in Context,* 40–54.

10. Myers, *Binding the Strong Man,* 310–14.

11. Herzog, *Parables as Subversive Speech; Prophet and Teacher.*

12. Lynda MacDonald, *www.angelfire.com/me4bread/h/lynda_fish.html.*

13. Malina and Rohrbaugh, *Social Science Commentary on the Gospel of John,* 293.

Chapter Eleven / What Empowering Discipleship Looks Like

1. See *www.westarinstitute.org/Jesus_Seminar/jesus_seminar.html.*

2. See Dunn, *Christianity in the Making,* 540; Schüssler Fiorenza, *Discipleship of Equals;* Tamez, *Struggles for Power in Early Christianity.*

3. See Crossan, *Jesus: A Revolutionary Biography,* 108ff.; Kaylor, *Jesus the Prophet,* 180.

4. Dunn, *Christianity in the Making,* 507–11.

5. Meier, "The Circle of the Twelve."

6. Crossan and Reed, *In Search of Paul,* xii–xiv.

7. Madden, *Jesus Walking on the Sea,* 35.

8. For more background information, see Witherington, *What Have They Done with Jesus?* 55–94.

9. Herzog, *Prophet and Teacher;* Horsley, *Jesus and Empire.*

10. Coffey, *Hidden Women of the Gospels,* 52ff.

11. Bauckham, *Gospel Women.*

Chapter Twelve / Empowerment as Women's Liberation

1. Borg, *Jesus: A New Vision,* 133–34.

2. Schüssler Fiorenza, *Discipleship of Equals.*

3. Corley, *Women and the Historical Jesus.*

4. Crossan, *God and Empire.*

5. Crossan and Reed, *In Search of Paul.*

6. Tamez, *Struggles for Power in Early Christianity.*

7. See Getty-Sullivan, *Women in the New Testament;* Schüssler Fiorenza, *In Memory of Her;* Tamez, *Struggles for Power in Early Christianity;* Thurston, *Women in the New Testament;* Witherington, *Women in the Ministry of Jesus.*

8. See D'Angelo, "Women in Luke-Acts"; Kraemer and D'Angelo, *Women and Christian Origins.*

9. Johnson, *Truly Our Sister.*

10. See Corley, *Women and the Historical Jesus.*

11. See *http://en.wikipedia.org/wiki/Mitochondrial_Eve.*

12. Wilton, *Sexual (Dis)orientation,* 112, 181.

13. Culpepper, "Seeing the Kingdom of God," and Reid, "Do You See This Woman?"

14. Bauckham, *Jesus and the Eyewitnesses,* 189ff.

15. For further background, see the essays by Gail R. O'Day and by Stephenson Humphries-Brooks in Levine, *A Feminist Companion to Matthew.*

16. Schüssler Fiorenza, *In Memory of Her,* 138.

17. Herzog, *Parables as Subversive Speech,* 231.

18. Carter, "Getting Martha Out of the Kitchen"; see also Fehribach, *The Women in the Life of the Bridegroom,* 83–113.

19. D'Angelo cited in Levine, *A Feminist Companion to Luke,* 242.

20. Schüssler Fiorenza, *In Memory of Her,* 144.

21. Myers, *Binding the Strong Man,* 315.

22. Van Voorst, *Reading the New Testament Today,* 178.

Chapter Thirteen / The (Dis)Empowerment of the Cross

1. See Heim, *Saved from Sacrifice*; Brock and Parker, *Saving Paradise*; Ray, *Deceiving the Devil*; Ruether, *Women and Redemption.*

2. Ruether, *Women and Redemption,* 279.

3. Dunn, *Christianity in the Making,* 775.

4. Malina and Rohrbaugh, *Social Science Commentary on the Gospel of John,* 256, 263.

5. Coakley, *Powers and Submissions,* 6ff.

6. See the informed analysis of Borg and Crossan, *The Last Week.*

7. Useful background material on Pilate in Bond, *Pontius Pilate in History and Interpretation.*

8. Malina and Rohrbaugh, *Social Science Commentary on the Gospel of John,* 264.

9. Brock and Parker, *Saving Paradise.*

10. Jantzen, *Becoming Divine.*

Chapter Fourteen / Resurrection as Cosmic Empowerment

1. Dunn, *Christianity in the Making,* 876.

2. See Fehribach, *The Women in the Life of the Bridegroom,* 143–67.

3. See Corley, *Women and the Historical Jesus.*

4. See Corley, *Women and the Historical Jesus,* 138.

5. Schüssler Fiorenza, *In Memory of Her,* 332.

6. E.g., de Boer, *The Mary Magdalene Cover-up*; George, *Mary Called Magdalene*; Graham Brock, *Mary Magdalene, the First Apostle*; King, *The Gospel of Mary of Magdala*; Schaberg, *The Resurrection of Mary Magdalene.*

7. For a useful resume see Ruether, *Goddesses and the Divine Feminine,* 122–26.

8. Madden, *Jesus Walking on the Sea.*

9. Crossan, *The Historical Jesus,* 404ff.

10. Meier, *A Marginal Jew,* 921.

Chapter Fifteen / Empowerment beneath the Language

1. Berry, *The Dream of the Earth*; *The Great Work*; Berry and Tucker, *Evening Thoughts.*

2. See Schneiders, *The Revelatory Text,* 180ff.

3. Malina and Rohrbaugh, *Social Science Commentary on the Gospel of John,* 98.

4. Further information in Fehribach, *The Women in the Life of the Bridegroom,* 45–81.

5. Benedict XVI, *Jesus of Nazareth,* 309.

6. See T. L. Donaldson (1985); K. C. Hanson, *www.kchanson.com/articles/mountain.html.*

7. Meier, *A Marginal Jew,* 933.

Chapter Sixteen / Empowerment through Human Solidarity

1. Armstrong, *The Great Transformation.*
2. See Amaladoss, *The Asian Jesus,* 108ff.
3. See Isherwood, *Liberating Christ,* 110ff.
4. O'Murchu, *Ancestral Grace.*
5. Marcus J. Borg: *www.beliefnet.com/author/author_52.html.*
6. See O'Murchu, *Ancestral Grace,* part 2.

Epilogue: Jesus, the Androgyne

1. See Singer, *Androgyny;* Vetterling-Braggin, *Femininity, Masculinity, Androgyny;* see also *www.Androgyne.0catch.com.*
2. See Harvey, *Son of Man,* 90ff.

Bibliography

Amaladoss, Michael. *The Asian Jesus.* Maryknoll, N.Y.: Orbis Books, 2006.

Armstrong, Karen. *The Great Transformation: The Beginning of Our Religious Traditions.* London: Atlantic Books, 2006.

Barclay, William, and John Drane. *The Gospel of Matthew: The New Daily Study Bible.* Vol. 1. Edinburgh: St. Andrew's Press, 2001.

Bauckham, Richard. *Gospel Women: Studies of the Named Women in the Gospels.* London and New York: T. & T. Clark International, 2002.

———. *Jesus and the Eyewitnesses: The Gospels as Eyewitness Testimony.* Grand Rapids, Mich.: Eerdmans, 2006.

Benedict XVI, Pope. *Jesus of Nazareth: From the Baptism in the Jordan to the Transfiguration.* New York and London: Doubleday, 2007.

Berry, Thomas. *The Dream of the Earth.* San Francisco: Sierra Club Books, 1988.

———. *The Great Work: Our Way into the Future.* New York: Bell Tower, 1999.

———, and Mary Evelyn Tucker. *Evening Thoughts: Reflecting on Earth as Sacred Community.* San Francisco: Sierra Book Club, 2006.

Bond, Helen. *Pontius Pilate in History and Interpretation.* New York and Cambridge: Cambridge University Press, 2004.

Borg, Marcus. *Jesus: A New Vision.* London: SCM Press, 1993.

———. *Meeting Jesus Again for the First Time: The Historical Jesus and the Heart of Contemporary Faith.* San Francisco: HarperSanFrancisco, 1994.

———, ed. *Jesus at 2000.* New York: Westview Press, 1999.

Borg, Marcus J., and John Dominic Crossan. *The Last Week: The Day-by-Day Account of Jesus's Final Week in Jerusalem.* San Francisco: HarperSanFrancisco, 2006.

Brandon, S. G. F. *Jesus and the Zealots: A Study of the Political Factor in Primitive Christianity.* New York: Charles Scribner & Sons, 1967.

Brock, Rita Nakashima, and Rebecca Parker. *Saving Paradise: How Christianity Traded Love of This World for Crucifixion and Empire.* Boston: Beacon Press, 2007.

Brown, Dan. *The Da Vinci Code: A Novel.* New York: Doubleday, 2003.

Brueggemann, Walter. *Hopeful Imagination: Prophetic Voices in Exile.* Philadelphia: Fortress, 1986.

———. *Finally Comes the Poet: Daring Speech for Proclamation.* Minneapolis: Fortress Press, 1989.

Bultmann, Rudolf. *New Testament and Mythology: And Other Basic Writings.* Minneapolis: Fortress Publishers, 1984.

Carter, Warren. "Getting Martha Out of the Kitchen: Luke 10:38–42 Again." *Catholic Biblical Quarterly* 58 (1996): 264–80.

Chatwin, Bruce. *Songlines*. London: Picador Books, 1988.

Coakley, Sarah. *Powers and Submissions: Spirituality, Philosophy, and Gender*. Malden, Mass., and Oxford: Blackwells, 2002.

Coffey, Kathy. *Hidden Women of the Gospels*. Maryknoll, N.Y.: Orbis Books, 2003.

Corley, Kathleen. *Women and the Historical Jesus: Feminist Myths of Christian Origins*. Santa Rosa, Calif.: Polebridge Press, 2002.

Crossan, John Dominic. *In Parables: The Challenge of the Historical Jesus*. New York: Harper & Row, 1973.

———. *The Historical Jesus: The Life of a Mediterranean Jewish Peasant*. San Francisco: HarperSanFrancisco, 1992.

———. *Jesus: A Revolutionary Biography*. San Francisco: HarperSanFrancisco, 1994.

———. *God and Empire: Jesus against Rome, Then and Now*. San Francisco: HarperSanFrancisco, 2007.

———, and Jonathan Reed. *In Search of Paul: How Jesus's Apostle Opposed Rome's Empire with God's Kingdom*. San Francisco: HarperSanFrancisco, 2004.

Culpepper, Alan. "Seeing the Kingdom of God: The Metaphor of Sight in the Gospel of Luke." *Currents in Theology and Mission* 21 (1994): 434–43.

D'Angelo, Rose Mary. "Women in Luke-Acts: A Redactional View." *Journal of Biblical Literature* 109 (1990): 441–61.

Davies, Steven L. *Jesus the Healer: Possession, Trance, and the Origins of Christianity*. London: SCM Press, 1995.

De Boer, Esther. *The Mary Magdalene Cover-up: The Sources Behind the Myth*. New York and London: Continuum, 2007.

Donaldson, Terence L. *Jesus on the Mountain: A Study in Matthean Theology*. JSNTSupplements 8. Sheffield: JSOT Press, 1985.

Douglas-Klotz, Neil. *The Hidden Gospel: Decoding the Spiritual Message of the Aramaic Jesus*. Wheaton, Ill.: Quest Books, 1999.

Dunn, James G. D. *Christianity in the Making*. Vol. 1: *Jesus Remembered*. Grand Rapids, Mich.: Eerdmans, 2003.

Edwards, Denis. *Jesus, the Wisdom of God: An Ecological Theology*. Maryknoll, N.Y.: Orbis Books, 1995.

Fehribach, Adeline. *The Women in the Life of the Bridegroom: A Feminist Historical-Literary Analysis of the Female Characters in the Fourth Gospel*. Collegeville, Minn.: Liturgical Press, 1998.

Fiand, Barbara. *From Religion Back to Faith: A Journey of the Heart*. New York: Crossroad, 2006.

Fox, Matthew. *One River, Many Wells: Wisdom Springing from Global Faiths*. New York: Jeremy P. Tarcher, 2000.

Fuellenbach, John. *The Kingdom of God: The Message of Jesus Today*. Maryknoll, N.Y.: Orbis Books, 1996.

Funk, Robert. *Honest to Jesus: Jesus for a New Millennium*. San Francisco: HarperSanFrancisco.

George, Margaret. *Mary Called Magdalene*. New York: Penguin Books, 2002.

Getty-Sullivan, Mary Ann. *Women in the New Testament*. Collegeville, Minn.: Liturgical Press, 2001.

Graham Brock, Ann. *Mary Magdalene, the First Apostle: The Struggle for Authority.* Cambridge, Mass.: Harvard University Press, 2003.

Groody, Daniel G. *Globalization, Spirituality, and Justice: Navigating a Path to Peace.* Maryknoll, N.Y.: Orbis Books, 2007.

Hanson, K. C. *Transformed on the Mountain: Ritual Analysis and the Gospel of Matthew*; see online *www.kchanson.com/articles/mountain.html.*

Harpur, Tom. *The Pagan Christ: Recovering the Lost Light.* Toronto: Thomas Allen Publishers, 2003.

Harris, Sam. *The End of Faith: Religion, Terror, and the Future of Reason.* London: Free Press, 2005.

Harvey, Andrew. *Son of Man: The Mystical Path to Christ.* New York: Jeremy P. Tarcher, 1998.

Hedrick, Charles W. *Many Things in Parables: Jesus and His Modern Critics.* Louisville: Westminster John Knox Press, 2004.

Heim, S. Mark. *Saved from Sacrifice: A Theology of the Cross.* Grand Rapids, Mich.: Eerdmans, 2007.

Herzog, William R., II. *Parables as Subversive Speech: Jesus as Pedagogue of the Oppressed.* Louisville: Westminster John Knox Press, 1994.

———. *Prophet and Teacher: An Introduction to the Historical Jesus.* Louisville: Westminster John Knox Press, 2005.

Hillman, James. *Archetypal Psychology.* Putnam, Conn.: Spring Publications, 2004.

Horsley, Richard A. *Jesus and Empire: The Kingdom of God and the New World Disorder.* Minneapolis: Fortress, 2003.

Housden, Roger. *Ten Poems to Change Your Life.* New York: Harmony Books, 2001.

Howard-Brook, Wes, and Anthony Gwyther. *Unveiling Empire: Reading Revelation Then and Now.* Maryknoll, N.Y.: Orbis Books, 1999.

Isherwood, Lisa. *Liberating Christ: Exploring the Christologies of Contemporary Liberation Movements.* Cleveland: Pilgrim Press, 1999.

Jantzen, Grace. *Becoming Divine: Towards a Feminist Philosophy of Religion.* Manchester: Manchester University Press, 1998.

Johnson, Elizabeth. *She Who Is: The Mystery of God in Feminist Theological Discourse.* New York: Crossroad, 1992.

———. *Truly Our Sister: A Theology of Mary in the Communion of Saints.* New York: Continuum, 2003.

Karris, Robert J. *Luke: Artist and Theologian.* New York: Paulist Press, 1985.

Kaylor, R. David. *Jesus the Prophet: The Rejected Prophet.* Louisville: Westminster/John Knox Press, 1994.

Kennelly, Brendan. *Selected Poems.* Dublin: Allen Figgis & Co., 1969.

Kersten, Holger. *Jesus Lived in India: His Unknown Life before and after the Crucifixion.* New York: Penguin, 2001.

King, Karen L. *The Gospel of Mary of Magdala: Jesus and the First Woman Apostle.* Santa Rosa, Calif.: Polebridge Press, 2003.

Klawans, Jonathan. "Moral and Ritual Purity." In *The Historical Jesus in Context,* ed. Amy-Jill Levine et al., 266–84. Princeton, N.J.: Princeton University Press, 2006.

Kloppenborg, John S. *The Tenants in the Vineyard: Ideology, Economics, and Agrarian Conflict in Jewish Palestine.* Tübingen, Germany: Mohr Siebeck, 2006.

Kraemer, Ross S., and Mary Rose D'Angelo, eds. *Women and Christian Origins.* Oxford: Oxford University Press, 1999.

Kraybill, Donald B. *The Upside-Down Kingdom.* Scottdale, Pa.: Herald Press, 2006.

Lee, Dorothy. *Flesh and Glory: Symbolism, Gender, and Theology in the Gospel of John.* New York: Crossroad, 2002.

Levine, Amy-Jill. *A Feminist Companion to Luke.* Cleveland: Pilgrim Press, 2004.

———. *A Feminist Companion to Matthew.* Cleveland: Pilgrim Press, 2004.

Levine, Amy-Jill, et al., eds. *The Historical Jesus in Context.* Princeton, N.J.: Princeton University Press, 2006.

Lüdemann, Gerd. *Virgin Birth? The Real Story of Mary and Her Son Jesus.* London: SCM Press, 1998.

Madden, Patrick J. *Jesus Walking on the Sea: An Investigation of the Origin of the Narrative Account.* New York: de Gruyter, 1997.

Malina, Bruce J. *The Social World of Jesus and the Gospels.* London: Routledge, 1996.

———, and Richard L. Rohrbaugh. *Social Science Commentary on the Gospel of John.* Minneapolis: Fortress Press, 1998.

Marshall, Christopher D. *Beyond Retribution: A New Testament Vision for Justice, Crime, and Punishment.* Grand Rapids, Mich.: Eerdmans, 2001.

McMaster, Susan. *Waging Peace: Poetry and Political Action.* Ottawa: Penmubra Press, 2002.

Meier, John P. *A Marginal Jew: Rethinking the Historical Jesus.* Vols. 1 and 2. New York: Doubleday, 1991, 1994.

———. "The Circle of the Twelve: Did It Exist during Jesus' Public Ministry?" *Journal of Biblical Literature* 116 (1997): 635–72.

Montefiore, Hugh. *The Miracles of Jesus.* London: SPCK, 2005.

Moule, C. F. D. "The Meaning of 'Life' in the Gospels and Epistles of St. John." *Theology* 78 (1975): 114–25.

Myers, Ched. *Binding the Strong Man: A Political Reading of Mark's Story of Jesus.* Maryknoll, N.Y.: Orbis Books, 1988.

Ogden, Schubert. *On Theology.* Dallas: Southern Methodist University Press, 1986.

O'Murchu, Diarmuid. *Catching Up with Jesus: A Gospel Story for Our Times.* New York: Crossroad, 2005.

———. *Ancestral Grace: Meeting God in Our Human Story.* Maryknoll, N.Y.: Orbis Books, 2008.

Perrin, Norman. *Jesus and the Language of the Kingdom: Symbol and Metaphor in New Testament Interpretation.* Philadelphia: Fortress Press, 1976.

Pilch, John J. *Healing in the New Testament: Insights from Medical and Mediterranean Anthropology.* Minneapolis: Augsburg Fortress, 2000.

Ray, Kathleen Darby. *Deceiving the Devil: Atonement, Abuse, and Ransom.* Cleveland: Pilgrim Press, 1998.

Reid, Barbara E. "Do You See This Woman? A Liberative Look at Luke 7:36–50." In Levine, *A Feminist Companion to Luke,* 106–20.

Reid-Bowen, Paul. *Goddess as Nature: Towards a Philosophical Thealogy.* Burlington, Vt.: Ashgate, 2007.

Reiser, Marius. *Jesus and Judgment: The Eschatological Proclamation in Its Jewish Context.* Minneapolis: Fortress Press, 1997.

Rosenblatt, Marie-Eloise. "Got into the Party After All: Women's Issues and the Five Foolish Virgins." *Continuum* 3 (1999): 107–37.

Ruether, Rosemary Radford. *Women and Redemption: A Theological History.* Minneapolis: Augsburg Fortress, 1998.

———. *Goddesses and the Divine Feminine: A Western Religious History.* Berkeley: University of California Press, 2005.

Rynne, Terence J. *Gandhi and Jesus: The Saving Power of Nonviolence.* Maryknoll, N.Y.: Orbis Books, 2008.

Schaberg, Jane. *Illegitimacy of Jesus: A Feminist Theological Interpretation of the Infancy Narratives.* New York: Harper & Row, 1987.

———. *The Resurrection of Mary Magdalene: Legends, Apocrypha, and the Christian Testament.* New York: Continuum, 2004.

Schimmel, Solomon. *Wounds Not Healed by Time: The Power of Repentance and Forgiveness.* New York: Oxford University Press, 202.

Schneiders, Sandra. *The Revelatory Text: Interpreting the New Testament as Sacred Scripture.* San Francisco: HarperSanFrancisco, 1999.

Schottroff, Luise. *The Parables of Jesus.* Minneapolis: Fortress Press, 2006.

Schüssler Fiorenza, Elisabeth. *In Memory of Her: A Feminist Theological Reconstruction of Christian Origins.* New York: Crossroad, 1985.

———. *Discipleship of Equals: A Critical Feminist Ekklēsia-Logy of Liberation.* New York: Crossroad, 1993.

———. *Jesus: Miriam's Child, Sophia's Prophet.* New York: Continuum, 1994.

Scott, James C. *Weapons of the Weak: Everyday Forms of Peasant Resistance.* New Haven, Conn.: Yale University Press, 1985.

Sheehan, Thomas. *The First Coming: How the Kingdom of God Became Christianity.* New York: Random House, 1986.

Singer, June. *Androgyny: Towards a New Theory of Sexuality.* New York and London: Routledge, 2000.

Song, C. S. *Jesus and the Reign of God.* Minneapolis: Augsburg Fortress, 1993.

Spencer, F. Scott. *What Did Jesus Do? Gospel Profiles of Jesus' Personal Conduct.* Philadelphia: Trinity Press International, 2003.

Tamez, Elsa. *Struggles for Power in Early Christianity: A Study of the First Letter to Timothy.* Maryknoll, N.Y.: Orbis Books, 2007.

Telford, William R. "The Barren Temple and the Withered Tree: A Redaction-Critical Analysis of the Cursing of the Fig-Tree Pericope in Mark's Gospel and Its Relation to the Cleansing of the Temple Tradition." *Journal of Biblical Literature* 101 (1982): 291–94.

Thurston, Bonnie. *Women in the New Testament: Questions and Commentary.* Eugene, Ore.: Wipf & Stock Publishers, 2004.

Untermeyer, Louis. *The Pursuit of Poetry: A Guide to Its Understanding and Appreciation with an Explanation of Its Forms and a Dictionary of Poetic Terms.* New York: Simon & Schuster, 1969.

Van Voorst, Robert. *Reading the New Testament Today.* Boston: Wadsworth Publishing, 2005.

Vetterling-Braggin, Mary. *Femininity, Masculinity, Androgyny: A Modern Philosophical Discussion.* Totowa, N.J.: Littlefield, Adams & Co., 1982.

Wallace, B. Alan. *Hidden Dimensions: The Unification of Physics and Consciousness.* New York: Columbia University Press, 2007.

Wiebe, Phillip H. *God and Other Spirits: Intimations of Transcendence in Christian Experience.* New York and Oxford: Oxford University Press, 2004.

Wilton, Tamsin. *Sexual (Dis)orientation: Gender, Sex, Desire and Self-Fashioning.* New York: Palgrave Macmillan, 2004.

Wink, Walter. *Naming the Powers: The Language of Power in the New Testament.* Philadelphia: Fortress, 1984.

———. *Unmasking the Powers: The Invisible Forces That Determine Human Existence.* Philadelphia: Fortress, 1986.

———. *Engaging the Powers: Discernment and Resistance in a World of Domination.* Minneapolis: Fortress, 1992.

———. *The Powers That Be: Theology for a New Millennium.* New York: Doubleday, 1998.

———. *The Human Being: Jesus and the Enigma of the Son of Man.* Minneapolis: Fortress Press, 2002.

Witherington, Ben. *Women in the Ministry of Jesus: A Study of Jesus' Attitudes to Women and Their Roles as Reflected in His Earthly Life.* Cambridge and New York: Cambridge University Press, 1987.

———. *Jesus the Sage: The Pilgrimage of Wisdom.* Minneapolis: Fortress Press, 1994.

———. *What Have They Done with Jesus? Beyond Strange Theories and Bad History — Why We Can Trust the Bible.* San Francisco: HarperSanFrancisco, 2006.

Wright, N. T. *Jesus and the Victory of God.* Minneapolis: Fortress, 1996.

About the Author

Diarmuid O'Murchu, author of the bestselling *Quantum Theology* and *Catching Up with Jesus,* is a member of the Sacred Heart Missionary Order and a graduate of Trinity College, Dublin, Ireland. He is a social psychologist whose entire working life has been in social ministry as a couples counselor, bereavement worker, and social worker with homeless people and refugees. As a workshop leader and group facilitator he has worked in Europe, the United States, Canada, Australia, the Philippines, Thailand, India, Peru, and in several African countries, facilitating programs on adult faith development.

Also by Diarmuid O'Murchu

CATCHING UP WITH JESUS
A Gospel Story for Our Time

In this sequel to *Quantum Theology,* O'Murchu shows us Jesus in a wholly new and creative way. He explains Jesus as the heart of the creative web of the universe and then offers imaginative dialogues and poetry that invite us to experience the wonder of the Quantum Christ.

"I find this book brilliant, liberating, and, most of all, truthful. O'Murchu presents us with a Christ worthy of the real one, a Christ who can lure humanity and history forward into a salvation that really feels like salvation — for all the peoples and all of creation."
— Richard Rohr, author of *Adam's Return*

ISBN 0-8245-2298-2, paperback

QUANTUM THEOLOGY
Spiritual Implications of the New Physics

Revised and Updated Edition,
with Reflective Questions

From black holes to holograms, from relativity theory to the discovery of quarks, an original exposition of quantum theory that unravels profound theological questions.

ISBN 0-8245-1630-3, paperback

crossroad

Of Related Interest

Richard Rohr
SIMPLICITY
The Art of Living

"Rohr's kind of contemplation is an adventure in the wilderness, letting God call me by name and take me to a deeper place of the peace that the world cannot give and can no longer take from one once it is encountered."   —*St. Anthony Messenger*

ISBN 0-8245-2115-3, paperback

Richard Rohr
EVERYTHING BELONGS
The Gift of Contemplative Prayer

Revised & Updated!

Richard Rohr has written this book to help us pray better and see life differently. Using parables, koans, and personal experiences, he leads us beyond the techniques of prayer to a place where we can receive the gift of contemplation: the place where (if only for a moment) we see the world in God clearly, and know that everything belongs.

"Rohr at his finest: insightful cultural critique—with strong connection to the marginalized."   —*The Other Side*

A personal retreat for those who hunger for a deeper prayer life but don't know what contemplation really is or how to let it happen.

ISBN 0-8245-1995-7, paperback

crossroad

Of Related Interest

Michael Crosby, OFMCap.
THE PARADOX OF POWER
From Control to Compassion

In religious settings, you can often hear people express distrust of power. But without power, nothing — evil or good — can be achieved. In this potent book, Michael Crosby draws from real-life examples and theory to explore the potential for inspiration and wisdom that resides in power, showing how the creative energy of power can heal and invigorate private relationships and institutional life.

Michael H. Crosby belongs to the Midwest Province of the Capuchin Franciscans. He holds a master's degree in economics, an STL, and a Ph.D. in theology. Fr. Crosby writes and speaks about biblical spirituality, while actively participating in the corporate responsibility movement, advising investors concerned about using their monies to promote social change. He is the author of several influential books, including the Catholic Press Award–winning *Can Religious Life Be Prophetic?*

ISBN 978-0-8245-2478-0, paperback

Check your local bookstore for availability.
To order directly from the publisher,
please call 1-800-707-0670 for Customer Service
or visit our website at *www.cpcbooks.com*.

crossroad